FAIR ENOUGH?

PINNER FAIR: THE LAST TWO HUNDRED YEARS

With best wishes Jim Golland APRIL 1993

Jim Golland

The Herga Press 1993

Dedicated to my wife; and to my Chiropractor, Cardiologist and Optician, who kept me going.

Copyright Jim Golland 1993

First published 1993

ISBN 1 - 873846 04 5

Origination and design: Beverley Bailey and Roger Bracey

Set in Times Roman & Switzerland

.

Printed by: Wilton Graphics, Salisbury

Published by The Herga Press
                3 London Road,
                Harrow on the Hill, HA1 3JJ

Cover photos:

Front   The Burger-Bar in front of The Queen's Head

Rear   The morning after: the High Street cleaned as dawn rises after the Fair.

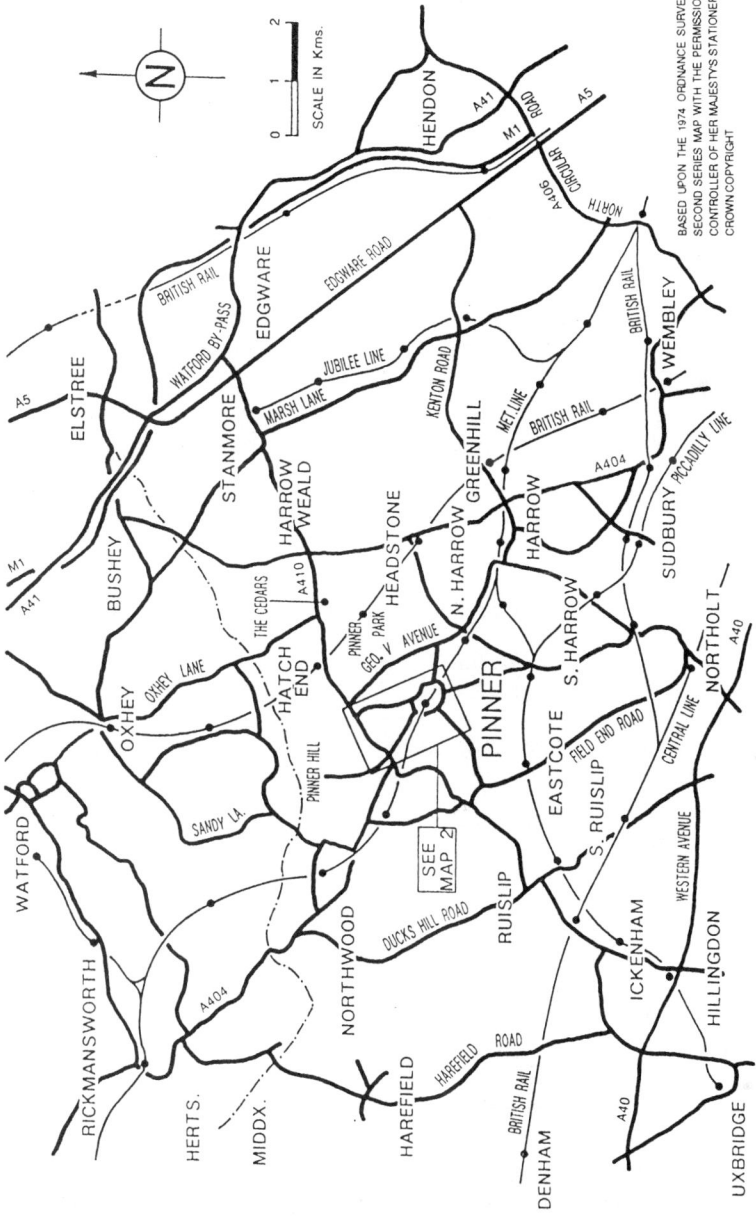

N

SCALE IN Kms.
0 1 2

A F VENIS

BASED UPON THE 1974 ORDNANCE SURVEY 1:50,000
SECOND SERIES MAP WITH THE PERMISSION OF THE
CONTROLLER OF HER MAJESTY'S STATIONERY OFFICE
CROWN COPYRIGHT

PINNER AND ITS NEIGHBOURS – MAP 1

3

Fair Enough?

CONTENTS

ILLUSTRATIONS

Colour photographs, including the cover, are by the author, and illustrate familiar scenes and horrifying fantasies from Pinner Fair in 1992. He also took the silhouette photograph on page 58.

The black and white photograph at the top of page 48 is by Mr W.Bentley; those on pages 48 (foot) and 73 by the Humphrey Saunders Studios; the remainder are from the collection in the London Borough of Harrow's Local History Library.

Black & white sketches are by Mr David Muriss

Fair Enough?

PREFACE

What was intended initially to be a one-page article was expanded into a pamphlet. Pressure for the abolition of the Fair at Pinner made further research imperative. The result is this tribute from a "josser" to all the Riding Masters and their helpers who have thrilled thousands over the years in our village street. In facing up to the problems raised by the Fair, I have tried to be as objective as possible, leaving readers to make up their own minds.   JG

ACKNOWLEDGEMENTS

In the course of my research I have had help from many people, some of whom are listed below. To them and all the many anonymous voices I tender my warmest thanks. Anyone researching Fairgrounds must be indebted to the late David Braithwaite for his splendid books on the subject. Especially am I grateful to Mr R Thomson of the Harrow Local History Library, for making available the files of the *Harrow Gazette* and the *Harrow Observer* as well as unveiling many other mysteries in his care such as the *Pinner in the Vale* collection of Edwin Ware. Mrs P A Clarke of the Pinner Local History Society has produced a new and complete translation of the Fair Charter and has discovered our earliest documentary reference to the Fair's existence. Her article on the Fair in *The Villager* for March 1986 expresses more succinctly the facts set out at length in this book.

I must thank, too, Mr G Peter Barnes of *World's Fair* for guiding me through the terminology of the fairground; Mr & Mrs D Rowlands, without whom none of this would have been possible; Mr R M L Bracey and Mrs B Bailey for the origination of the type-setting; Mr D Muriss & Mr A F Venis for illustrations and maps; the staff of the Eastcote Library; and my wife, for her unfailing support and tolerance.

In the cause of legibility, I have kept footnotes to a minimum, but a fully annotated edition of the book will be placed in the Harrow Reference Library. I am grateful to the following for giving permission to print extracts from their books, papers or manuscripts:

Mr R Thomson, Local History Librarian, Harrow for archive material and some black and white photographs, Mr Peter Saunders of the Humphrey Saunders Studios, Pinner, and Mrs Bentley for other photographs;

Malvern Publishing Co (for extracts from *Fairfield Folk* by Frances Brown);

Metropolitan Police (Harrow);

World's Fair for extracts from their issues in 1907, 1935 and 1952;

HM Stationery Office, The Ordnance Survey and Public Record Offices at Kew and Chancery Lane;

City of London Corporation, for material at the Greater London Record Office;

The Editor of *The Harrow Observer, and* Mr H Rockwell (for extracts from *The Villager*).

My grateful thanks are due also to the members of the following institutions for their help:

The Pinner Local History Society and its Research Group, The Pinner Wood Middle School, The Greater London Record Office and History Library, Hillingdon Borough Branch Libraries at Ruislip and Uxbridge, Harrow Borough Branch Libraries at Harrow and Pinner, The Showmen's Guild: London and Home Counties Section (Sec.: Mrs Morris), The Newspaper Library, Colindale, The British Library, The Guildhall Library, The General Register Office (St. Catherine's House), London Borough of Harrow Engineering Department

and to the following individuals:

Mrs E Bowlt, Mrs A Brown, Mrs B E Chase, Mr O Cock, Mrs L Darley, Mr C G Ellement, Mr G Ensten, Mrs I Field, Mrs C Flint, Mr B Harrison C B E, Ms Charlotte Hastings, Mr K Kirkman, Mr & Mrs P Long, Mrs Maplestone, Mr & Mrs K Maurice, Mr H J Mees, Miss H Moodie, Mr & Mrs D Muriss, Mr J Oldfield, Mr W Parslow, Mr K Pearce, Mrs Marion Percy, Mr L Perrin, Mr H Rockwell, Miss K Sharp, Mr D Thompson, Rev D Tuck, Mr P Turnell, Mr & Mrs A F Venis, Mr D Walter, Mrs Wardell, and Mr G Young of Nova Scotia

and to the writers of the books mentioned in the Bibliography, as well as the Editors of: *The Times, The Daily Mirror, The People, The Buckinghamshire Advertiser and Gazette, The Harrow Gazette, Panorama of Pinner Village*

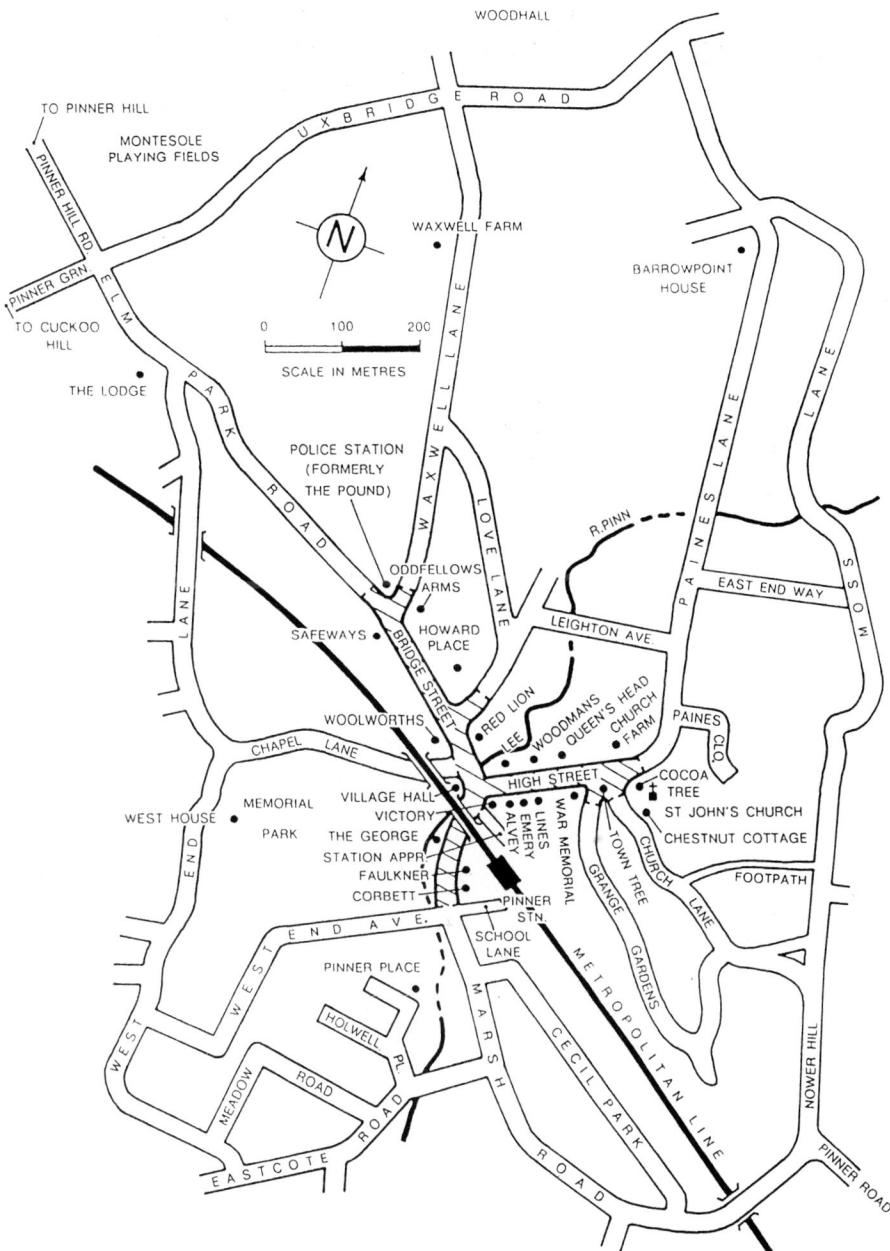

WOODHALL

UXBRIDGE ROAD

TO PINNER HILL

MONTESOLE
PLAYING FIELDS

WAXWELL FARM

BARROWPOINT
HOUSE

PINNER HILL RD

PINNER GRN

TO CUCKOO
HILL

THE LODGE

ELM PARK ROAD

WAXWELL LANE

LOVE LANE

PAINES LANE

MOSS LANE

N

0   100   200

SCALE IN METRES

POLICE STATION
(FORMERLY
THE POUND)

R. PINN

EAST END WAY

ODDFELLOWS
ARMS

LANE

SAFEWAYS

HOWARD
PLACE

BRIDGE STREET

LEIGHTON AVE.

WOOLWORTHS

CHAPEL LANE

RED LION

LEE

WOODMANS
QUEEN'S HEAD

CHURCH
FARM

PAINES
CLO.

HIGH STREET

COCOA
TREE

ST JOHN'S CHURCH

WEST HOUSE

MEMORIAL
PARK

VILLAGE HALL
VICTORY

THE GEORGE
STATION APPR.
FAULKNER
CORBETT

LINES
EMERY
ALVEY

WAR
MEMORIAL

CHESTNUT COTTAGE

FOOTPATH

TOWN TREE

CHURCH LANE

GRANGE

PINNER
STN.

SCHOOL
LANE

WEST END AVE.

PINNER PLACE

HOLWELL
PL

METROPOLITAN LINE

GARDENS

NOWER HILL

WEST END

MEADOW ROAD

EASTCOTE
ROAD

MARSH ROAD

CECIL PARK

PINNER ROAD

PINNER – MAP 2

THE FAIR STREETS SHOWN HATCHED

A F VENIS

Fair Enough?

INTRODUCTION

THE ROMANCE OF THE FAIRGROUND: Some Literary extracts

PINNER FAIR

About twelve miles from London Town
A little village stands,
In quiet lanes for shady walks,
And pleasant meadow lands.
It is a homely little place
As anyone can see;
But still there's great improvements
On what it used to be.

And in the height of Summer time
Men come from far away,
And all day in the scorching fields
They work, all making hay;
Now once a year we have a Fair,
It makes the streets quite gay,
And to the Pinner people
It is quite a crazy day.
The children dressed in all their best
Are at the stalls all day.

For till their money is all spent
They cannot come away;
And many a quiet old couple
Will leave their homes to see
The young folk all enjoy the fun
As happy as can be.

It is the only holiday
We have in all the year
And is looked forward to for months
By many children near;
Of course, there's discontented folks
And village gossips too,
Who spread ridiculous rumours,
And tales both false and true.

But 'tis no idle tale they tell,
Its truth shows more and more
That Pinner Fair has enemies,
Who have often tried before.
And try to stop it every year
With all their might and main;
But every Whitsun Wednesday yet
It has appeared again.

Though now it seems as if success
In part their efforts meet,
To try to pass an act that Fairs
Shall not be in the street,
But there are still some gentlemen
Who bear the Fair good will;
Among the two or three I know
Is Mr. D—— H——.[1]

He's promised our folks a field
In which to hold their sport,
And so its enemies' hard trials
Will all be brought to nought;
Now may our people long enjoy
Their well known yearly treat.
And in the fun next year I hope
All my good friends to meet.

JULIA ISABELLA BUGDEN
(Aged 13) 1868
(From E M Ware, *Pinner in the Vale* Collection)
(By permission of Harrow Reference Library)

Oh! you should see us go
Round the blooming show,
The village all aglow
With lamps of naphtha.

Oh! you should see us pay
The showmen's fare:
It's a terrible price,
But awfully nice
At good old Pinner Fair.

(Song, c.1905, quoted by E M Ware in *Pinner in the Vale*, para 292)

1. Daniel Hill (see page 82)

And the music breaks into bright pieces, and joins together again, and again breaks, and is dissolved, and the crowd scatters, moving slowly up the hill. At the corner of the road the stalls begin.

"Ticklers! Tuppence a tickler! 'Ool 'ave a tickler? Tickle 'em up, boys."

Little soft brooms on wire handles. They are eagerly bought by the soldiers.

"Buy a golliwog! Tuppence a golliwog!" "Buy a jumping donkey! All alive-oh!"

"Su-perior chewing-gum. Buy something to do, boys." "Buy a rose. Give 'er a rose, boy. Roses, lady?"

"Fevvers! Fevvers!" They are hard to resist. Lovely, streaming feathers, emerald green, scarlet, bright blue, canary yellow. Even the babies wear feathers through their bonnets.

(From *Bank Holiday* in *Collected Stories* of Katherine Mansfield (Constable 1945)

* * * * *

At present, as their informant had observed, but little real business remained on hand, the chief being the sale by auction of a few inferior animals, that could not otherwise be disposed of, and had been absolutely refused by the better class of traders, who came and went early, yet the crowd was denser now than during the morning hours, the frivolous contingent of visitors, including journeymen out for a holiday, a stray soldier or two come on furlough, village shopkeepers and the like, having latterly flocked in; persons whose activities found a congenial field among the peep-shows, toy-stands, waxworks, inspired monsters, disinterested medical men who travelled for the public good, thimble-riggers, nick-nack vendors, and readers of Fate.

(Thomas Hardy, *The Mayor of Casterbridge* Ch.1. (McMillan)

* * * * *

Autolycus: Lawn as white as driven snow;
Cyprus black as e'er was crow;
Gloves as sweet as damask roses;
Masks for faces and for noses;
Bugle-bracelet, necklace- amber;
Perfume for a lady's chamber;
Golden quoifs and stomachers,
For my lads to give their dears;
Pins and poking-sticks of steel;
What maids lack from head to heel;
Come buy of me, come: come buy, come buy;
Buy lads, or else your lasses cry;
Come buy.

Clown: He hath ribands of all the colours i' the rainbow .... no milliner can so fit his customers with gloves.....

Mopsa: Come, you promised me a tawdry[2] lace and a pair of sweet gloves.

(Shakespeare: *The Winter's Tale* :Act IV Sc.3)

2. See page 50

9

Fair Enough?

With silver, iron, tin and lead they traded in thy Fairs......They of the house of Tagarmah traded in thy Fairs with horses and horsemen and mules.......they traded in thy Market wheat.....honey, oil and balm......wine... and white wood....precious clothes for chariots.....lambs and rams and goats.....they occupied in thy Fairs with chief of all spices and with all precious stones and gold.....in chests of rich apparel bound with cords and made of cedar.....

(Ezekiel, Ch.27)

* * * * *

No learned-pig, no veal, no mutton pie,
No heads be crack'd, no undergarments won,
No giants twelve, no dwarfs just three feet high,
No calves with two heads shown to calves with one.

(From *Elegy on the Death of Bow Fair*
quoted by William Addison, *English Fairs and Markets* (Batsford 1953))

* * * * *

John Masefield shows the other side of the coin, the hardships of the life led by the travellers:

In all my tour along the river's reaches
I've had ill-luck; I've clashed with public feasts.
At Wycombe Fair we met performing beasts,
At Henley, waxworks, and at Maidenhead
The Psyche woman talking with the dead.
At Bray, we met the rain, at Reading, flood,
At Pangbourne, politics, at Goring, mud.

(From *King Cole* in *Selected Poems* of John Masefield (Heinemann, 1978))

(Edward Fuller wrote a poem about Pinner Fair during fire-watching duty in June 1941. It can be read in *Panorama of Pinner Village*)

PATRONISED BY HIS MAJESTY The PUBLIC

Above   The Fair in Pinner High Street 1929
showing the famous carousel, the swings and the coconut shies.

Left   Typical showman's humour.

Fair Enough?

CHAPTER 1

"THE BUILD-UP"

COME TO THE FAIR

Roll up! Roll up! All the fun of the Fair!

The blood tingles, the excitement mounts, as we realise that our annual holiday and festival has arrived. Gone are the workaday clothes. It is on with the new bonnet and shoes and hey-ho off to the Fair.

Coarse, bawdy, noisy and odorous, the Fair generates a holiday-postcard kind of atmosphere. Staid old Pinner lets her hair down, kicks off her shoes, lifts up her skirts and dances a fandango. It is low, sleazy, blowsy and deplorable, but it is fun.

The highly-charged excitement that crowds produce gives Pinner Fair a special flavour that is increased by its location. Crammed together in a small space, laughing and dancing in the main streets of the village where normally we buy our bread and butter and dodge the cars, we feel for a brief moment liberated and uplifted.

Once a year the festival takes over, the Mardi Gras of Middlesex, the charabanc trip, the music hall, the seaside outing, the cheap tawdriness of glitter and tinsel, candyfloss and toffee-apples, loud music and showmen's banter. Once in the year we indulge ourselves in becoming part of something greater, a crowd in search of pleasure.

The confetti battles that took place before the last war at Pinner Fair were witnesses to the extraordinary spirit of the day - the pleasure of the Fair came, dare we say it, as much from being in the throng as from anything the stalls had to offer. We knew the freaks were tricks, we knew the prizes were often second-rate; but at the end of the pier, who cares? "Pinner Fair was the biggest excitement of our lives," said a villager in 1980, looking back on an Edwardian childhood.

Today, the youth of Pinner and district are more sophisticated and have unimaginable opportunities for fun and excitement, without even leaving home. Video games and TV can transport them in an instant to the far ends of the earth or onto the Moon. Fantasy games release their imaginations. Alton Towers and Thorpe Park provide artificial excitements for them until they become motor-cyclists or aeroplane pilots themselves. A young man years ago mounted a horse on a roundabout to try to experience some of the thrills of horse-riding, which he probably could not afford. Later came roundabouts with trains or cars to help him imagine other delights beyond his purse. But nowadays he has flown to Marbella, dived under the sea with a snorkel, and ridden in a flight simulator at the Royal Tournament. Small wonder, then, that he and his sister crave from their visit to a Fairground something more than a magic roundabout, that they must be flung out and up and around and upside down whilst all the time revolving at tremendous speed. Small wonder that the rides at Pinner Fair get larger every year.

The lovely, romantic, cosy, jolly Fair of yesterday is perhaps a thing of the past.

The authorities now - those who would get the blame if anything untoward happened - are becoming increasingly concerned about the growing size, not of the Fair itself, which is kept strictly within the bounds of the shopping centre, but of some of the rides. Modern technology is making ever more spectacular devices for those who crave excitement; but there comes a time when the constraints imposed by the location of the Fair between rows of shops in a suburban street must be considered.

That this concern is nothing new is shown in Chapter IV, where the reasons for complaints about the Fair are discussed and in Chapter V, where the various protests since 1829 are listed. Those who value the Fair as a tradition that marks Pinner out from other suburban villages must think about possible solutions. Changes of taste and changing economic patterns are bound to affect the strange organisation that is Pinner Fair.

Do we want it to return to the earlier Cattle Fair, with its attendant smell and manure, or merely to swings and roundabouts like a playground in a recreation ground? Do we want it to stop altogether? Do we want it to be moved to a playing field far from the reach of public transport?

The latter suggestion is receiving some support as we write. A similar suggestion was made in 1920; but Mr. G C Ellement on that occasion pointed out that in a field there would be no street lights, which do at least provide a modicum of security. There would also be no water hydrants in case of fire. If it were to rain on Fair Day (and it has been known: see page 75) imagine the state of the playing field such as Montesole after it had been traversed by a hundred lorries and tramped over by 200,000[3] people. What would the Cricket Club think if their field drains were cracked by lorries? And where is the atmosphere in a bleak open field?

Economics demand that showmen cram as many people as possible onto a ride for a relatively short time. Their period for trading is limited to the summer season and to a few days in each week - Hampstead Heath, perhaps, on Whit Monday, Pinner on the Wednesday and Rochester or Epsom on the Friday. A ride holding forty people is to be preferred to one holding four. They are not entirely altruistic, coming to Pinner merely for the sake of maintaining tradition, though, with Beaconsfield, they reckon Pinner to be one of the best one-day Fairs in the land.

How then do we resolve this dilemma? Public opinion and the good sense of the Showmen's Guild working in collaboration with Health and Safety Officers and the Council must surely find an acceptable compromise.

3. This figure is the latest estimate by the Police of how many people pass through the Fair in one twelve hour period.

Fair Enough?

THE FOUNDATION

It is generally agreed by historical authorities that the granting of a royal charter merely confirmed an existing situation: so it seems likely that Markets had been held at Pinner, with perhaps a grander one every year worthy of the name of "Fair" for some years before King Edward III on 30th May 1336 granted to the Lord of the Manor of Harrow in the person of the Archbishop of Canterbury (possibly in return for some financial consideration or merely as an act of piety to save his own soul) the right to hold a Fair on five days a year at Pinner and at Gillingham and Thanet in Kent. Among other towns granted Charters in 1336 were Helston in Cornwall and Tamworth and Newcastle in Staffordshire. As he already had permission for a Market in Harrow, the Archbishop was perhaps looking for ways of augmenting his income. The tolls from anyone selling goods at a Market could be quite substantial.

M R Price in her book, *A Portrait of the Middle Ages*, says that at that time traders at a Fair in Derbyshire paid a penny for bringing in a cartload of produce, a halfpenny for a horse-load, and a farthing for a man-load. Stalls would be hired out to traders at perhaps twelve pence a day; even a site to stand or sit and sell her eggs would cost a farmer's wife twopence. That might be as much as a week's rent for a reasonable land-holding. A serving man at that time might have earned £2 a year.

In 1441 the Archbishop of Canterbury is said to have remitted all Market tolls for his Harrow tenants: it is thought that this may possibly be because of their discontent in losing the woods in which they fed their pigs, when the former were cut down for the building of All Souls' College, Oxford (1438-43).

Tolls were certainly still being collected in the 19th century. In 1859 the Beadle of Harrow parish was instructed by the Lord of the Manor not to collect any tolls' from the Harrow Fair on August 1st, following complaints about it from local inhabitants.

In the Middle Ages there were some Fairs in Britain that were so large they were known all over Europe, and traders would come from distant parts to sell spices, salt, wine, cloth, furs, silk, almonds, sugar loaves, (then a great delicacy), ginger, pearls or live animals and birds.

Among these larger Fairs were those at St Ives, in Huntingdonshire, Winchester (which lasted three weeks), Stourbridge, near Cambridge (started by King John in 1211 and closed in 1927). St Bartholomew's Fair in Smithfield (1133 - 1855), St Botolph's at Boston, Lincs, and Northampton. The Nottingham Goose Fair was given its Charter in 1284 but was a relatively small affair for the sale of birds until it took off as a Pleasure Fair in the last century. It seems doubtful, however, that silk merchants from Damascus or carpet sellers from Turkey would ever have found their way to Pinner Fair.

THE CHARTER OF PINNER FAIR - 30TH MAY 1336

Transcribed and translated by Patricia Clarke from the copy of the charter shown in *Pinner in the Vale* Vol III p. 168 by E M Ware, and adapting the translation of part of the same therein, and that part of a transcription and translation by the P.R.O. given in *The Villager* No. 164 p.16.

For John Archbishop of Canterbury

The King to the same[4] greeting - Know ye that of our special grace we have granted and by this our charter confirmed to the venerable Father John Archbishop of Canterbury and Primate of all England that he and his successor Archbishops of the said place forever may have one Market each week on Monday at his manor of St Nicholas in Thanet in the county of Kent and one Fair there each year for two days duration that is on the morrow of the Nativity of the Blessed Virgin Mary and on the day next following and one Market each week on Thursday at his manor of Gillyngham in the said county and one Fair there each year for eight days duration that is on the day of the Finding of the Holy Cross and for seven days next following Unless that Market and that Fair are to the detriment of neighbouring Markets and neighbouring Fairs And therefore we will and firmly order for us and our heirs that the said Archbishop and his successors aforesaid shall have in perpetuity the said Markets and Fairs at his said manors with all liberties and free customs to the said Markets and Fairs belonging Unless they are as aforesaid These being witnesses the venerable fathers Henry Bishop of Lincoln our (Treasurer) Richard Bishop of Durham John Earl of Cornwall our most dear brother William of Montacute Robert of Ufford steward of our household and others Given by our hand at Wodestok 30th day of May

The King to the same greeting Know ye etc. as above as far as 'forever may have' and then thus - one Market each week on Wednesday at his manor of Pynnore in the county of Middlesex and two Fairs there each year for five days duration one that is on the vigil and the morrow of St. John the Baptist and the other on the day and the morrow of the Beheading of St. John the Baptist Unless etc. as above as far as the end The witnesses being as above. Given as above

By the King himself and by writ of privy seal

The entry in the Calendar of Charter Rolls IV 1327-41 p.360 is as follows:

May 30 Woodstock

Grant of special grace to John Archbishop of Canterbury and his successors of a weekly Market on Monday at their manor of St. Nicholas Thanet co. Kent and a yearly Fair there on the morrow of the nativity of St. Mary and the following day; of a weekly Market on Thursday at their manor of Gillyngham co. Kent and a yearly Fair there on the feast of the Invention of the Holy Cross and the seven days following and of a weekly Market on Saturday[5] at their manor of Pynnore co. Middlesex and a yearly Fair there on the vigil the feast and the morrow of the Nativity of St. John the Baptist.

---

4   "The same" refers to those greeted in an earlier charter in the Roll, namely the Archbishops, Bishops, Abbots, Priors, Earls, Barons, etc.

5   The day of the Pinner Market has been wrongly translated in the Calendar; the correct day is Wednesday - *diem mercur.* Two Fairs, not one, were granted: P.A.C.

Fair Enough?

WHO SIGNED THE CHARTER?

King Edward III, the warrior king, interested above all in chivalry and martial pursuits, fought wars against Scotland and, from 1337, the year after the Charter, against France. This struggle continued, long after his death, for a hundred years in all, while England sought to establish its right to rule France. Edward was the son of Isabella of France, daughter of the French king and nicknamed "the she-wolf of France", and it was through her that he and his successors claimed the throne of France, a claim that they reinforced by putting the arms of France in the prominent position in the Royal Arms: these fleurs-de-lys appeared there until they were eventually dropped in 1801, when Britain ceased at last to claim the right to the by then non-existent French monarchy.

Edward III is remembered as the chivalric founder of the Order of the Garter; but he was also the cause of much hardship among the poor through the taxes he imposed to pay for his wars. He reigned from 1327 - 77, and it was during the latter part of his reign that Langland wrote *The Vision of Piers the Plowman*, which graphically describes the lot of the peasantry groaning under a heavy economic burden. Eventually, after Edward's death, the peasants rose in anger and Edward's young grandson, Richard II, had to face the Peasants' Revolt in 1381.

The Charter was granted to **John Stratford**, Archbishop of Canterbury 1334 - 48. He was the man who established Headstone Manor as his palace in 1344. He had been Treasurer or England (the predecessor of our Chancellor of the Exchequer) in 1326, when he was Bishop of Winchester. He was Chancellor of England and Keeper of the Great Seal in 1330, 1335 -37 and 1340.

The witnesses to the signing, who were all members of the Privy Council, were led by **Henry Burghersh**, Bishop of Lincoln 1320 - 40. (A kinsman of his, Bartholomew, 1st Baron de Burghersh, was Keeper of Pinner Park in 1349). The Bishop was Treasurer in 1327 and from 1334 - 37. He was Chancellor in 1328.

Another witness, **Richard of Bury St. Edmunds** was Bishop of Durham 1333 - 45. He too had held great offices of State, being Keeper of the Privy Seal 1329 - 34, Treasurer for a few months in 1334 and Chancellor in that same year when Stratford was briefly out of office. He was a great lover of books, and was said to have had a larger library than all the other bishops put together.

First among the laymen was the king's own brother, **Prince John of Eltham**, who had been made Earl of Cornwall in 1328. (The Prince of Wales is now Duke of Cornwall). Born at Eltham Palace in 1316, John survived only a few more months after witnessing the Charter: in September of 1336 he died fighting the Scots at Perth. His mother the "she-wolf" is shown as one of the "weepers" engraved on the side of his tomb.

William de Montagu (or Montacute) was Steward of the Manor of Woodstock, where the Charter was signed. He had been made a Privy Counsellor in 1330, and was the founder of Bisham Abbey, near Maidenhead. At the start of the Hundred Years War in 1337 he was made Earl of Salisbury.

Another lord so ennobled at that time was **Robert de Ufford**, who became Earl of Suffolk. At the time of the Charter, he was Steward of the Household, an informal title that seems to have been granted by word of mouth: documentary evidence for the appointments of Stewards is sadly lacking. He was born in 1298, the 2nd Baron de Ufford and Warden of the Royal Forests in the south of England, and was one of the first of the Garter knights, being used frequently as an ambassador in delicate negotiations with foreign monarchs. He died in 1369. Like Salisbury, he had been made a Privy Counsellor in 1330. His Arms can be seen in a window in Montacute House in Somerset.

(With acknowledgements to *The Handbook of British Chronology* (Royal Historical Society 1961) and *Who's Who in History* by W O Hassall (Blackwell 1960)

PINNER AND THE MIDDLE AGES

1260/61	Harrow Fair founded
1273	First mention of Pinner Park in a document as part of lands owned as the Archbishop of Canterbury
1314	Local residents illegally felled the trees of the Archbishop of Canterbury in Pinner Park
1321	Consecration of re-built Pinner Church by Bishop Peter of Corbavia
1323	Fences round Pinner Park broken
1327	Edward III came to the throne
1336	Edward III granted Charter establishing weekly Market and five Fair Days a year to Archbishop Stratford at Pinner, Thanet and Gillingham, Kent.
1337	Hundred Years War started
1344	Archbishop Stratford took over Headstone Manor
1346	Battle of Creçy
1348	The Black Death; two keepers appointed for Pinner Park. (Baron de Burghersh in 1349)
1356	Battle of Poitiers
1377	Edward III died and was succeeded by Richard II
1381	Peasants' Revolt
1399	Richard II deposed and murdered. Henry IV King of England
1438-43	Building of All Souls' College, Oxford, with trees from Harrow Manor
1441	Archbishop said to have remitted market tolls to tenants in Harrow Manor

WHY ON JUNE 24TH?

Pinner Parish Church is dedicated to St. John the Baptist, whose birth is celebrated on June 24th. It is probable that the Saint's Nativity would have been celebrated by a service in the church in the morning, followed by some sort of recreational activity in the afternoon and, possibly, a feast. The Charter perhaps merely confirmed existing practices by granting permission for the Archbishop to hold a Fair on the day of St. John's Nativity and the day either side.

William Addison even suggests that Fairs are of such antiquity that it is possible that in dedicating a church to a particular saint, care was taken to choose one whose festival was closest in date to that of an existing Fair. Ox-roasting, he suggests, may derive from pagan burnt offerings.

The word "fair" derives, said the Royal Commission of 1889, not from *forum*, a market-place, but from *feria*, a proper ecclesiastical word for a saint's day. Early records show that gatherings on saints' days were used not only for religious purposes, but for trade, commerce and pleasure. Some early laws forbade the sale of cattle other than at a Fair or Market.

THE SITE

It should be noted that the Charter founding Pinner Fair grants the right to the Archbishop as Lord of the Manor to hold a Fair at Pinner on certain days: it does not specify a location. Lawyers agree that the holder of the rights of the Fair or Market has the right to move it to another situation within his Manor. They do not agree, however, as to who owns Pinner Fair nowadays.

In many towns and villages across the country, Fairs have been traditionally held in the streets. The presence of many beasts in the middle of a village was often thought to be unhygienic and a considerable public nuisance, and strong efforts were made in many places to remove them. The tradesmen, however, realised that Fairs brought in trade and made equally strenuous attempts to keep them. Their struggles are recorded in Chapters V and VI.

WHY WHIT-WEEK?

The Charter laid down the dates of the Fair as being 23rd - 25th June and 29th - 30th August, but at some stage these dates were changed. The Markets fell into disuse, the second Fair was abandoned (if it had ever taken place) and the Fair on the eve, day and morrow of the birth of St. John the Baptist was altered to the Wednesday of Whit-week.

The change could have taken place following the passing of the Fairs Act in 1448, but this does not seem likely. That Act forbade the holding of Fairs on Sundays and on "principal feasts" such as Ascension Day, Whit Sunday, the Feast of Corpus Christi or All Saints. (see page 97). It does not specifically ban Fairs on Saints' Days. It is possible that the date was changed when the calendar was altered in 1752 and ten days were lost. It was certainly not being held on June 24th in 1769 (see page 22).

The day chosen was in fact an Ember Day, a day of fasting.

Following the prolonged fasting of Lent, the fifty days up to Pentecost had given time for Mediterranean people to gather in the harvest and be aware of the gifts of God: the Ember Days of Whit-week gave time for reflection and the expressions of gratitude. Peter's sermon on Pentecost urges, "Your sons and daughters shall prophesy. Your young men shall see visions and your old men shall dream dreams." (Acts ch.2.v.17).

Those words seem to suggest that the Wednesday of Whit-week was as good a time as any for a Fair, with "shows, fortune tellers and trials of strength."

"And when the day of Pentecost was fully come, they were all with one accord in one place." (Acts ch.2, v.1)

"Now when this was noised abroad, the multitude came together...." (ib. v.6.)

"And I shall show wonders in heaven above, and signs in the earth beneath; blood and fire and vapour of smoke ..." (ib. v. 20)

As the Whit-week Ember Days were therefore to celebrate the harvesting of wheat, the bread of life and also the harvesting of souls by the Holy Ghost, it was more a time of rejoicing than of penance and would be a fitting time for a Fair.

"EVERY FAIR IS A MARKET BUT NOT EVERY MARKET IS A FAIR" (Legal definition)

"A FAIR IS A KIND OF LARGE MARKET HELD AT LONG INTERVALS AND HAS ALWAYS BEEN ASSOCIATED WITH ENTERTAINMENT AS WELL AS WITH THE BUYING AND SELLING OF ANIMALS AND GOODS." (ditto)

Fair Enough?

PRESS REVIEWS

WHAT PEOPLE HAVE SAID ABOUT PINNER FAIR

1   The Tradition

The green but Arcadian simplicity of the good old days...   (1885)

Ye Good Olde Fayre of Pinner   (1896)

A heritage not to be despised; unless roustabouts start heaving bricks through Pinner windows, nothing seems likely to end Pinner Fair   (1925)

So far, not even national calamities have broken its run   (1939)

Now it was ....somehow stimulating....both for the continuity of its tradition and for its challenge to the view that there's little to do in life save go to the office on the 8.44 and return on the 5.6   (Howard Spring 1943)

Here is a scene as old as our country's history and as typical of our way of life as the craftsmanship that goes into the products of the Standard Motor Co., representing as they do in every detail of their design "All that's best in Britain."
                                                                                (Advertiser's Announcement 1950)

The Fair - noted in America as one of Britain's major tourist attractions   (1950)

From Hampstead Heath the Fair folk move into Pinner High Street at Whitsuntide with their booths and roundabouts, with the result that these lively examples of ancient Fairs in modern dress, adorned as they are with all the spangles and trappings of the traditional Fair, and with pearly kings and queens to lead the revels, preserve in the twentieth century the spirit of Dickensian Greenwich and of the immemorial Bartholomew (William Addison 1953)

I think the Fair should go on for ever   (Pinner shopkeeper 1985)

Without the Fair, Pinner would be no different from a great number of other villages swallowed up in London's sprawl   (1986)

Pinner Fair is part of Pinner and should never be removed from the village   (1992)

2   Its Function

It is a reunion for old inhabitants, those friends and relations who have left Pinner but return annually for this occasion, for a dinner of roast pork or goose   (1890)

A wonderful safety valve   (1939)

A meeting place for Trendies   (1976)

It's a day out for the family   (1984)

In the 14th century, it was a sort of bucolic job-centre   (Derek Sankey 1985)

3   Those in Favour

The Fair is looked upon by the youth of Pinner as a red-letter day   (1881)

The whole village puts on quite a holiday appearance   (1881)

On Wednesday the village of Pinner rose from its semi-somnolent tranquillity and rang apace with the harmonious and rattling strains of steam organs, the persuasive shouts of hawkers and showmen, the laughter and joyous shouts of merry-makers in playful and sportive mood   (1923)

We were always given a holiday from the National School for the Fair. Bridge Street was turned into Laughtermakers' Lane   (1939)

The best one-day Fair in England   (1952)

Judged by the showmen to be one of the finest Fairs in Britain   (1954)

Into the normal humdrum activities of the village, shopping, the business of living, came a fast-moving bomb, which exploded right in the centre: the ancient Pinner Fair. It exploded into a thousand pieces among Fair barkers, relaxed crowds from far and wide, shouting and revelling in the thrills to be bought there. It was a bomb full of laughter, candy floss and toffee apples, spinning carousels and plunging rides.   (1960)

A dazzling arena of fun and games   (1989)

As a little girl, I was given a new dress every year to wear to the Fair   (1992)

4 The Uncertain

This more or less welcome fixture....   (1904)

With its attendant contrast of old-world charm and modern amusement   (1924)

The Fair is a great annoyance to the residents close to the main street, a lesser annoyance to others further away, and a delight to 20,000 visitors   (1934)

Pinner's greatest Pride or greatest Pest...   (C A Lejeune 1950)

A bugbear for the residents, a magnet for the showmen, and a thrill for the young in heart
                                                                               (1976)

5 The Slightly Derogatory

A scene of the wildest noise and tumult   (1885)

The Fair was attended by crowds of the middle and lower classes   (1888)

This has degenerated into an insignificant Pleasure Fair   (1898)

This noisy, untidy, archaic institution   (1934)

The raucous, alcoholic breath of life...   (1943)

Pinner went quite berserk   (1960)

A shanty-town of death-defying rides   (1966)

Flashy, faintly sleazy and totally unnecessary   (1980)

The bustling blaring bedlam of today's monster machines whirling the masochistic merrymakers around with mind- (and stomach-) turning momentum   (D Sankey 1985)

6 The Jeremiahs

Pinner Fair is said to be played out   (1887)

This is the last Pinner Fair   (1914)

It has outlived its useful purpose   (1925)

This year may be the last of its kind   (1934)

Fair Enough?

MYTHS

Pinner Fair has attracted to itself a number of legends, some of which may be true, although proof is lacking or has not yet been uncovered. In the course of research, one comes across statements like these:

1. "Pinner Fair was granted by Edward III to give thanks for the Battle of Creçy, as the bows used there were made from trees in Pinner Woods."

   (The Battle was fought ten years after the Charter.)

2. "The Fair was granted by the Archbishop of Canterbury to compensate the villagers for the loss of pannage (the right to feed pigs in woodland) caused by the felling of trees for the building of All Souls' College, Oxford, which he had founded."

   (a: The Fair was granted by the King <u>to</u> the Archbishop

   (b: The grant was a century before All Souls was built

   (c: Archbishop Chichely in the 15th century may have remitted tolls on Harrow Fair for such a reason, though no firm evidence has come to light).

3. "The Fair is owned by the people of Pinner, and any ratepayer can put up a stall." (M Darvell, in *Time Out* 23rd May 1980). "There is a Royal Charter given to the people of Pinner, not Harrow." (Edwin Ware). "The inhabitants of Pinner alone can claim ownership of Pinner Fair." (Edwin Ware, *Harrow Observer* 5th November 1971)

   (See page 14). (The Charter was given to the Lord of the Manor of Harrow, allowing him to collect tolls from stallholders. As land ownership in the 20th century is different in kind from that in 1336, it is difficult to say who does now "own" the Fair. Even if doubts about the details of transfer in 1547 are resolved (see page 120) there is no Lord of the Manor at present. The Charter granted a Fair for five different days from the one on which it is now held, so its relevancy has been questioned, but it is generally agreed that long usage "since time immemorial" confers rights and privileges irrespective of any charter. Anyone putting up a stall on his own account would face the wrath of the showmen, who pay a rent for their pitches, and of the Council, who receive it)

4. "The Fair has been held every year since 1336."
   (The traditional view could well be true; but firm evidence is woefully lacking. Would the Commonwealth have allowed it, for instance? Why does William Owen not list it in his *Book of Fairs* in the eighteenth century? A small Cattle Fair at the top of the High Street would not attract much notice though, and the absence of documentary evidence is not necessarily surprising. He does not refer to Harrow Fair, either. He does ask proprietors of Fairs to let him know of errors or omissions. Clearly, Lord Northwick never bothered. Mrs. P A Clarke, of Pinner Local History Society, has found our earliest reference to it so far, when William Bodimeade, a local brickmaker, recorded an expenditure of 7/- (35p) at Pinner Fair in 1769, where he seems to have bought a quantity of wine.)

5. "The Fair was held annually on Whit Monday" (*The Villager* 6)

   (Originally in June and August (see page 15); later changed to Whit Wednesday. When that change was made is not known.

6. "The Saturday Fair was held in the field at the top of the High Street." (Watford paper, 1881) (Dated in *The Villager* 46 as 1887)

   "The Saturday Fair was considered rough, so we went mid-week." (Contemporary reminiscence of pre-war days.)

   "In the 19th century it was held on two days." (Henry Dyer, in *The Villager* 43)

   (Confirmation is still sought)

7. "For the buying and selling of cattle and merchandise." (Poster in 1894)

   (It seems unlikely that cattle were still being sold at so late a date. The poster was probably a response to the attempt to ban the Fair in 1893 by suggesting it was other than merely a Pleasure Fair (see page 112)

8. "The second Fair (in August, see page 15) was abandoned in the 18th century." (Writer in 1980)

   "The second Fair was dropped about 1835." (*World's Fair* 1935)

   "The second Fair was defunct by 1876." (*The Villager* 144)

   (Someone must be wrong. Mrs Clarke thinks it possible that it never started).

9. "A showman's wife had a daughter at the Fair just before the war. She was baptised by the Vicar, Rev C E Rowlands." (Newspaper reports 1984) "It was a boy and he was baptised by Rev Elliott." (Informant 1992)

   (Percy Pinner Buckland was born 9th June 1933 and baptised by Rev P D Ellis - see page 68)

10. "The Home Secretary came to the Fair in 1894 to see for himself."

    (See page 112). If he did, he had already made up his mind not to ban the Fair. In any case, the local paper was remarkably quiet about this event.)

11. "The Charter provided that should the Fair not be held in any year the right to hold it thereafter would be forfeited." (Letter to *Harrow Observer* 3rd June 1965)

    (No such requirement in the Charter)

12. "Pinner has always been quite separate from Harrow, manorially." (Letter to *Harrow Observer* 1971)

    (Pinner was always part of the Manor of Harrow).

Fair Enough?

THE RUSH-IN

For many, whose tastes do not run to noisy music and being whirled around at vast speed, the best part of the Fair is the evening before. Motorists are warned not to park near the centre of the village and to leave the station car park by lunch-time. At 4 p.m. police arrive with lorries to tow away any vehicles still left parked in Bridge Street or the High Street. Some showmen arrive and mark the pavements to show the extent of their pitches. Shopkeepers hurriedly lock their doors and load essentials into cars. A husband waits impatiently outside McDonalds as his wife collects the evening take-away. He is told by police to move on, but fears his wife's wrath if she comes out to find him gone.

There is a pause. A Burger-bar lorry parks in the car-park of the Queen's Head. Young men who will scarcely stop working for the next 36 hours sit idly in the afternoon sun under the chestnuts of Church Farm.

Crowds gather to watch. The atmosphere is tense, like something from "High Noon". A stall holder, waiting for her husband to be allowed into the village, nods in a doorway. She has been up all the Monday night after Hampstead Fair. A postman dashes in to clear the box in Grange Gardens.

Bus shelters, litter bins and zebra refuges are removed. All is quiet. Still we wait.

Meanwhile, in George V Avenue, lines of caravans and lorries wait for permission from the police before they move any nearer.

Five o'clock strikes. The Burger-bar moves out from behind the Queen's Head. Two motor-cycle police roar up Bridge Street as if heralding a royal cavalcade. The lorries have arrived.

All is chaos. Early arrivals start reversing trailers to use as the driving force for roundabouts, and block the entrance of others. Tempers flare. They want to get the work done before the pubs close. Baulks of timber are laid out to form the basis for a ride. A trailer is manoeuvred with incredible skill to within an inch of the Waxwell Lane road sign.

The council men keep a wary eye open for infringements of space. The Showmen's Guild are on hand to settle any disputes. Stalls are unfolded, tilts unwrapped. From cardboard boxes appear hundreds of stuffed toys. The fair is taking shape.

Long before midnight, all is ready.

* * * * * * *

In former days, the first sign of the approaching Fair for many residents on the fringes of the village was the arrival of the horses to graze in nearby fields or on grass verges after they had deposited their caravans or trailers. West End Lane was a favoured place, and as far away as Grubb's Field near Fore Street in Eastcote, pasture was occupied by the travellers' animals (see page 81). In one field by "The Ship" in Joel Street, showmen used to open up their stalls the day before the Fair and on the days afterwards until interest waned or neighbours complained.

> "Hearing the galloping of hooves along Bridle Road, children would hurry down to the village to savour the excitements of the stalls being unpacked and the roundabout horses emerging from their cocoons like gaudy butterflies."

At four or five or six oclock, or even midnight (according to changing fashion or fallible memories) the maroon would sound from the police station or the sergeant would blow a whistle, and the rush-in or 'drawing in' would start, with stall-holders striving to reach the best positions. Formerly they would have placed a pole in the gutter beforehand to mark their pitches, but in many years before the war, fights occurred when poles were moved and disputes arose. To upstage their colleagues, showmen started arriving earlier and earlier: the need to be first on the spot meant that they were occupying the nearby roads for hours beforehand.

During the war, regulations were relaxed and for some years afterwards there were complaints from residents about lorries arriving early, and parking outside front gates. There was noise and the barking of dogs and the dropping of poles (see page 87).

In 1947 it was early on Tuesday morning; by 1951 they were arriving on Monday night. Before the war, there was not quite so much urgency as the Fair did not really get going until after noon on the Wednesday.

The Showmen's Guild maintained that many of those arriving prematurely and causing disturbance were not in fact their members.

Their problems were compounded before the war as traffic was allowed through between the stalls and the current traffic diversions were not in place. Until the 1960s, Green Line coaches had to thread their way through the throngs (see page 80).

The growing frequency of these complaints led to the Council taking over the arrangements. In November 1957 and again in May 1958, the Guild met the representatives of the Council and formulated a plan to organise the entry into the village. By 1961, parking in George V Avenue only was allowed, with windscreen labels issued to the showmen in 1962 and coloured routes for entry in 1963.

Contrary to popular belief, however, there is nothing in the Charter that lays down the hours by which the showmen must leave the village. All arrangements are done by agreement with the police and the Council.

Before the war, Tuesday evenings must have been bell-ringing practice night at the church. One resident recalls as his abiding memory of the Fair hearing the church bells pealing out a welcome as he hurried down to the village to see the men setting up their stalls.

SPECIAL VISITORS

From time to time, someone of note has visited the Fair. To celebrate the 600th anniversary in 1936, there was a gathering of famous authors, when Howard Spring, who lived in East End Way, invited A J Cronin and Dennis Wheatley, together with their wives, to savour the delights of our festival. In 1951, the cast of the show "Count Your Blessings", then running at the Westminster Theatre, came to the Fair at the invitation of their producer, Stanley French of West End Avenue. They were headed by the stars of the show, Naunton Wayne and Joyce Redman, who enjoyed a ride on the helter-skelter outside the Red Lion and on the nearby carousel. Mr Wayne won two prizes on the Round Table darts stall. Ten years later, an honoured visitor was 101-year-old Frederick Pitt.

Two Police Inspectors from Hong Kong were taken round the Fair in 1980 to see our methods of crowd control, and were duly impressed.

According to William Addison (*op.cit.*), the Pearly King and Queen used to make regular visits. Herbert Asquith is reputed to have attended in 1894, but no evidence of this has yet been found (see page 112).

The BBC descended on Pinner in 1958 to record a ten-minute programme in their Town and Country feature on the Home Service. Several local personalities and some of the showmen were interviewed. The recording is still being traced. In 1961, the Fair featured on TV in the Town and Around programme. Charles Maplestone of Aspect Films made a film in 1966 about two people meeting at the Fair. Again, it is still being tracked down. The Pinner Cine Society do still have the films they have made, including one sequence recording the blissful scene on the morning after, with a spotless High Street denuded of cars.

CHAPTER II

"THE TOBER"

THE EARLY YEARS

What was Pinner Fair like in its early days?

The short answer is that we do not know. We know indeed very little about the first four hundred years of the Fair, apart from the granting of the Charter by the King authorising the Lord of the Manor to hold it in 1336.

From other areas we can see that mediaeval man celebrated the official birthday of the patronal saint with a holiday, in which he attended a service at church in the morning and engaged in sporting contests in the afternoon. It is interesting to note that until very recently, Pinner Fair did not start until the afternoon, though this may latterly have been more to do with shop closing hours than with church services.

In the Middle Ages, mass football matches took place in some parishes; in others archery was the communal sport. This latter was encouraged by the Crown, as helping to train men in the skills necessary for the defence of the realm. Maintaining the butts was a charge on the parish purse.

Early forms of other martial arts would be practised, too, such as cudgel play or quarter-staff fighting. Any activity that enabled men to show their strength or agility was popular, such as hammer throwing, wrestling or boxing. The present Highland Games give an indication of the kinds of pursuit likely to be followed on these occasions, though the particular fashions would change over the centuries and from area to area.

Probably by that time farmers had been bringing in their cattle and sheep to be sold in the space at the top of the High Street, on what was possibly a village green. It may have been reserved for the purpose and may account for the size of the area and explain why the High Street seems to open out towards the top. The Fair every year would be larger than the weekly Market, but could not have been too large or it would have interfered with trading at the markets at Harrow or Uxbridge.

As crowds gathered to inspect the livestock, no doubt villagers hung a green bush outside their cottages to show that they would supply refreshment to the farmers. Perhaps housewives would bring out examples of their craft work, such as their smocking, to show and sell.

A fiddler might play for villagers to dance a jig. Jugglers, tumblers, acrobats, fire-eaters, illusionists[6] or conjurors would arrive, travelling from Fair to Fair across the

---

6   One of the 18th century fairground attractions was an illusionist who presented "The Decollation (Beheading) of St. John the Baptist." Cunningly placed cloths and a table with two holes allowed two men to present an apparent beheading, with the severed head of the Baptist seen on a dish. Surely this would have been popular at Pinner in the shadows of St. John's Church? In 1888 "The Original Bosco", the Royal illusionist, appeared at the Public Hall in Harrow with "The Beheading of a Living Lady with her Head on a Plate." (Harrow Gazette 23rd September 1888)

south of England. Buskers might arrive to entertain the crowds after the chaffering had been done. Strolling minstrels and travelling players would deploy their lutes or set up a stage to act out a drollery. Pedlars would display "fairings" - ribbons, laces or other knick-knacks unobtainable locally. "He promised he'd bring me a bunch of blue ribbons," goes the song; though it is noticeable that the young lady singing it and worrying what has delayed her Johnny has not felt it seemly to go to the Fair herself. Simple Simon met a pieman going to the Fair, where no doubt he would do good trade.

Animal trainers would bring along their dancing bears, performing dogs or intelligent horses to amaze the peasants.

When the Puritans objected to all this frivolity, the Fairs probably returned for a time to their original function as Cattle and Trade Fairs only. Perhaps not until the nineteenth century and the growth of permanent shops did the Trade Fairs wither, to be taken over by amusements.

To get some idea of what Pinner Fair was like early in the 19th century, we can turn to Thomas Frost in *The Old Showmen and Old London Fairs*, where he describes Croydon Fair at that time. Amongst the detailed description he gives, he mentions the cattle, sheep and horses being sold on the first day, to be followed by the Circus, with its lion tamer, tight-rope-walker and fireworks; the Menagerie, run by Wombwell, with its attractive painted canvas screen outside; two theatrical companies with Pantaloon and Harlequin; young ladies in muslin skirts dancing; combats with broad swords; and three refreshment salons. Of these, the "Crown and Anchor", famous for fifty years, was patronised by the better class of shopkeeper and farmer for dancing to the harp and violin. The boxing fraternity and their like favoured the "Fives Court". The least select establishment, but the most romantic, was the Gipsies' Booth, with Romany waitresses with long ear pendants, flashing eyes and wicked ways. Outside this booth was the green bough as a sign that beer was on sale. There was also a quadrille band.

Plentifully supplied at Croydon were gingerbread stalls, and sellers of walnuts, oysters and sausages. Waxworks presented scenes from history. The only Fairground entertainments familiar to us would have the swings, roundabouts and "Knock'em Downs", with three shies for a penny (though not yet for coconuts). Gongs, speaking trumpets and dance music made a din, and at night the place was transformed by thousands of lamps in blue, amber and green, arranged in patterns of stars, crowns and anchors to illuminate the booths.

But we must leave Uncle Tom Cobbleigh and all riding their grey horse to Pinner Fair, because this is all in the imagination. We know it happened elsewhere and the chances are that it happened here, too. The visitors to Pinner Fair left little documentary evidence of their activities. No doubt some will be unearthed in due course, but this study is concerned only with the years that do have some evidence, those of the 19th and 20th centuries.

Younger researchers, with more years ahead and time to spare, may trawl through records in search of proof that Pinner Fair did exist for all those four hundred years. All we know is that when Mr. Owen recorded all the Fairs of Britain in the eighteenth century (and his book ran to several different editions) he unaccountably forgot to include Pinner. So did the Royal Commission on Market Rights and Tolls in 1889. When St. Bartholomew's Fair was having its doings recorded by Ben Jonson, no playwright came to our streets to savour the delights of roast pork or puppet shows; but in the 1830s it was famous enough for boys at Harrow School to want to break bounds to come to enjoy its festivities.

And that is where we start.

ALL THE FUN OF THE FAIR

By 1830 Pinner Fair was sufficiently well established for the Edgware magistrates to want to ban it (see page 98) and for Harrow schoolboys to brave their masters' wrath by escaping from their boarding houses in order to visit it. There they would either accept the challenge of a round with a boxing champion or simply ride in the swingboats.

The Rev. Henry Torre was at Harrow School from 1832 to 1838. In his recollections of his schooldays, he wrote about Pinner Fair:

> "Harrow wake or feast day took place in the Summer holidays but Pinner Fair was celebrated about the longest day of Summer, when the lads and lasses of the whole village were let loose in the evening.
>
> Several of the Harrow boys used to attend. We used to go across the fields, about four miles, to Pinner. There were booths and stalls in a small way. The chief attractions were roundabouts, swinging-boats, single-sticks and boxing matches; among the labourers, jumping in sacks, climbing a greased pole for a leg of mutton or a hat on the top, and last but not least in importance a dance at a public house.
>
> We left Harrow about four or five o'clock in the evening and I well remember one evening, when the Fair was at its height, Dr. Longley (Head Master 1829 - 36), who probably had his suspicions aroused, rode through the village. Our boys hid and ran into nooks and corners, but one of the boys, whose nickname was Butcher, happened to be in a swingboat at the time and so could not run away, but with adroitness hid himself among the petticoats of his companions and Dr. Longley rode close to him without seeing him.
>
> The dancing was in a small room and the atmosphere, impregnated with the smell of beer and tobacco, and the noise of the dancing in chaw boots to a merry fiddle were something indescribable. Dancing continued till about midnight, when we walked back to Harrow. I remember day dawning on us before we got to our respective houses."

This is a most valuable eye-witness account, as it clearly shows that the pleasurable activities of Fair Day were at least by the 1830s looming large. The dancing must have

29

PINNER FAIR.

According to Ancient Custom

founded upon a charter, granted to the Lord of the Manor, and his successors, by King Edward the 3rd, in the 10th year of his reign, 1337.

A Fair will be Held at Pinner,

FOR THE BUYING AND SELLING OF

CATTLE

AND MERCHANDIZE,

On Whitsun-Wednesday,
The 25th of May, 1831.

In the course of the Day, Prizes will be offered for Wrestling, Foot Racing, Gingling, and other manly and old English Sports.

For Pens, Standings, &c. apply to William Dean, Pinner.

W. Lowe, Printer, 37, New Compton street, Bloomsbury.

been very exhausting, since it took them over four hours to walk as many miles back to school. ("Chaw" was their word for a yokel: one wonders which inn suffered the pounding of the iron shod boots of local labourers enjoying the antic hay.)

Swings and roundabouts, the traditional elements in any Fair, are seen to be already present. The boat swings continued in use until very recently.

SPORTS

The 1896 Fair was reported as having as one of its main attractions an Assault-at-Arms, though what form this took is not clear. Whether one merely watched two fencers in action or had a chance to engage in a more sophisticated kind of single-stick is not stated. Single-stick was a kind of fencing, using a stick provided with a basket to protect the hand. It was a later refinement of the mediaeval sport of quarter-staff fighting.

Later reminiscences, too, speak of the greased pole. Sometimes the mutton would be "off" and a money prize would be given instead. Thomas Ellement, born in 1877, recalled the greasy pole in the yard of The George in Marsh Road. A dead duck was tied to a branch suspended over a pond and the prize for releasing it without falling in the water was a leg of mutton or a pound of tea. George Barter, born much earlier, in 1841, remembered the competition as being organised by James Dean.

It is, though, interesting to see the persistence of this kind of test of skill that also gives pleasure to the spectators: an early predecessor, perhaps, of "It's A Knock-out".

A further piece of contemporary evidence is the handbill advertising the Fair in 1831, published in *Panorama of Pinner Village*: it suggests that the main purpose of the Fair was still the selling of cattle, as mentioned by John Smart and his friends in their petition (see page 98), but it adds that during the day prizes would be offered for wrestling, foot racing, gingling and other "manly and old English sports". Gingling was a reversed form of "blind man's buff", in which the players were all blindfolded except for one, who ran around an enclosed space ringing a bell in each hand while the others tried to catch him.

Another handbill, eight years later, is more detailed and lists a series of races and contests. There is the greasy pole to be climbed for a leg of mutton, outside the George just as it would be fifty years later. At the old Red Lion (now Red Lion Parade, on the corner of Love Lane), there was another popular feature of many old Fairs: the eating competition, an activity still indulged in by people wanting to enter the Guinness Book of Records. In 1839, contestants had to eat rolls and treacle. Presumably it was a question of the maximum number in a given time (or possibly the shortest time for a given number of rolls). Drinking a yard of ale or hastily eating hot puddings or other signs of cast-iron digestions, have long been popular at country Fairs and Fêtes.

Wheelbarrow races also feature on this 1839 handbill: they were said by the editor of *Panorama of Pinner Village* to be derived from the old plough races, though with what authority is not known.

31

Fair Enough?

The wheelbarrow races were for people who were blindfolded: like the greased pole, the sport was no doubt hilarious for the spectators. Such races are still a means of local fund-raising, with contestants having to patronise a number of pubs on their circuit.

The main activity, though, was a series of foot races. Their routes were given, and the fact that competitors were expected to run (with varying handicaps) between the Queen's Head, the town tree (which until 1898 stood at the top of the High Street), the George, the Red Lion and the village pound (now the site of the police station) suggests that the roads could not have been too cluttered with swings, roundabouts and stalls. As late as the 1890's, Edwin Ware tells us of the annual race along Marsh Road, up Nower Hill and Church Lane to the High Street. The winner received the "Town Plate" (see page 78). In 1890 a local worthy, one-armed "Turk" Nash, won a bet by walking forty circuits of the course in twelve hours, an average of just under 3 m.p.h.

In view of the long tradition of ladies' pancake races, it is interesting to see that one of the races was for "six females", to be chosen as the best from preliminary heats. The boys' race had to be run backwards, from the George up the High Street to the Queen's Head and back: no mean feat. The men had no handicaps, but for one race had to pay an entrance fee; their races were longer, too.

For all these, handsome prizes were offered, possibly by pub landlords attracting custom, but these were traditional in Fairs all over the country: pancake race winners too, used to be given a new smock. The ladies' prize of a pound of tea was a considerable luxury in those days. The men's prizes of a silver watch, or a new whip, were sure to attract a good number of entrants.

Included in the races is a donkey race. Rides, if not races, on donkeys and ponies long remained a popular feature of the Fair. Sites on the fringes were usually chosen where there was open space, in Paines, Church, School, Chapel, Love or Waxwell Lanes. For a penny (3d in 1939) you could ride from Bridge Street up Chapel Lane to the railway bridge and back. The rides were not always without incident (see page 84). The Donkey Derbies of the 1930's were merely recreating an old Pinner custom.

The last item, a duck hunt, strikes a more ominous note, but again reflects the coarser susceptibilities of an earlier age. Only a hundred years or so earlier, Shrove Tuesday had been celebrated at Pinner with the barbarous sport of throwing sticks at tethered cockerels, in order to raise money for the church. Details of the duck hunt are lacking; ducks may have been released in a field and chased by terriers, the owner of the successful dogs being able to keep the prize. The duck hunt was one of the prime attractions at the original May Fair held near Hyde Park. There, a duck sat on a pond and dived below the water to escape the dogs. At Harrow later in the last century, rats were released for dogs to chase them.

Children sometimes chased rabbits that were let loose among the crowds, or competitors had to catch with one hand a greased piglet with a docked tail - there would be few winners. There were crueler sports, too, like biting the head off a tethered sparrow, or, whilst blindfolded, trying to whip a hen in a basket.

PINNER FAIR,

ON

Wednesday May 22nd 1839,

WITH A

VARIETY OF PLEASING

AMUSEMENTS.

1st.—To Wheel a Barrow (each person Blind-folded,) from the Queens Head Inn, to the Town Tree and back into the Yard, for a New Smock Frock, to be turned round once before starting.

2nd.—A pound of Tea to be Run for by Six Females, from the Red Lion, to the Town Tree and back,—best of Heats.

3rd.—A Donkey Race for a New Bridle, from the Town Tree to the Parish Pound, and back to Queens Head,—best of Heats.

4th.—A Silver Watch to be Run for by Men, from the Red Lion, to the Town Tree and Back,—to pay 6d. entrance,—best of Heats.

5th.—To Climb a Pole for a good Leg of Mutton, at the George Inn.

6th.—Eating Rolls and Treacle at the Red Lion, for a New Hat.

7th.—A New Whip to be Run for, by Men, from the Town Tree to the Parish Pound, and Back to the Queens Head.

8th.—A New Waistcoat to be run for backwards, by Boys, from the George to the Queens Head and back.

9th.—To wheel a barrow (each person blind-folded,) from the Red Lion, to the Queens Head and back, for a New Flannel Jacket.

10th.—A Duck Hunt, &c. &c.

J. PEACOCK, PRINTER, WATFORD.

Fair Enough?

Akin to the greasy pole was the ducking pond, in which a boy would be tipped from his stool into the water when a ball hit its target: at Fêtes in this century his place would have been taken by a girl being tipped out of bed.

According to Henry Dyer, landlord of the Red Lion in Bridge Street, who was born in 1860, the Fair in his youth took place on the Tuesday and Wednesday of Whit week, and included "the traditional sports events that were still a feature of village festivities."

In 1910 the local paper commented that "this was not the Fair of fifty years ago, when there were few stalls, and village sports were held in the main street."

From other sources, we can imagine that the attractions at the Fair during the first half of the last century might have included "gurning", that is grinning through a horse collar and making unattractive faces; whistling while others tried to make you laugh; and sack races (the "jumping in sacks" mentioned by Torre). There were still sack races at Harrow Fair in the 1850s.

Rope-dancers, stilt-walkers, jugglers, acrobats, conjurers, fire-eaters and sword-swallowers have for centuries been the mainstay of Fairgrounds; and the festivities would be a magnet for dancing bears, mountebanks and quack doctors offering cure-alls.

THROWING

Games of skill, however, persisted. Customers have long been asked to test their skills, not so much in racing as streets became more congested, but in throwing, rolling, shooting or thumping. From the sticks thrown at cocks developed the more harmless coconut shy. The OED notes its first appearance in 1879 and a photo of Pinner Fair dated 1885 shows the shy in full swing.

A report of the Fair in that year referred to the ear-splitting cries of the coconut men, a recurrent theme in later accounts. "The neatly poised coconuts invited the skill of the young men," continued the writer. In 1904 young women as well were seen to try their hand, though in the rather rowdy Fair of 1901, the shies had seemed to be losing their popularity, being "neglected while the public houses were full". A slogan in a 1936 photo of a shy in Bridge Street reads. "We find the nuts; you find the whoopee!"

Just before the war, coconuts were four shies for sixpence (2½p) and "many a young man carried home coconuts for the lady of his choice, who no doubt disposed of them as soon as conveniently possible."

Proprietors of coconut "sheets", as they are known, were much respected in the profession - men like Tom Fitzpatrick, King Nut in 1911.

Coconuts disappeared during the last war, and the return of real nuts was greeted with enthusiasm in 1950.

In many of the pictures of the Fair, the name of Smith appears prominently over the shies advertising "Continental Cokernuts". In 1929, for instance, O. Smith, Jane

COKERNUTS!
COKERNUTS!

BRINKLEY'S

CELEBRATED

COKER NUTS!

THE LARGEST AND BEST ARE THE CHEAPEST

Write for Price List, to

BENJAMIN BRINKLEY & Co.

COKERNUT MERCHANTS

Mitre-St., Aldgate, LONDON, E.8

Above Advertisement from *World's Fair* 1907.
Below Pettigrove's roundabout with swings and coconuts in 1885.

Fair Enough?

Smith and A. Smith had stalls near The Queen's Head. Nelson Smith in 1961 said he had been coming for 44 years and he was the third generation of his family to do so. The Smith family of Belvedere in Kent were on the same site in 1992.

For over a hundred years the coconuts have held their own as one of the major attractions of the Fair, and many a childhood has been enlivened by the noisy attempts to break through the hard shell without frightening the newly-won goldfish.

In 1938 the coconut stall near Waxwell Lane was causing trouble for buses trying to reverse into Bridge Street before returning to Northwood (see page 80), From time to time, whispers spread about how hard it was to dislodge the nuts even when they were hit, and malicious rumours circulated about the use of glue. "There appears to be a growing desire," said one report, "to make Pinner people scientists if they are to secure coconuts."

In the 1880s a popular stall for the throwers was the Aunt Sally, in which people were asked to throw a ball and knock down a cardboard cut-out. Originally the cut-outs resembled figures in the much derided Salvation Army, known colloquially as the "Sally Army"; but as the missionary work of the Army was seen to be necessary and the stalwart campaigners came to be tolerated and even admired, other figures were substituted. By 1885 the Aunt Sally figures were losing custom; by 1900 they had been replaced by Boer War villains. In 1906 the targets included Fussy Fanny, Pretty Jane and the Goalkeeper. Aunt Sally was still there in 1924, but regarded then as "time-honoured."

In recent years, we have been able to take out our spleen on Middle Eastern dictators or unpopular politicians. The tradition of the village stocks dies hard.

Various other missiles were used occasionally, such as a bundle of rags to knock down piled up cans or snuff boxes. Sometimes "livetts" were used. These were sticks eighteen inches long. In Victorian days, dummies would have clay pipes in their mouths, which would have to be knocked out by the livetts. In the wrong hands, the sticks made quite formidable weapons, as at the fight recalled by "Lord" George Sanger between two rival gangs of gipsies at Moulsey Races in 1836. When the fight was interrupted by the police, the gipsies turned on them with dire results.

A rather more genteel sport is the throwing of a ping-pong ball into a goldfish bowl or similar receptacle. It proves extraordinarily difficult to stop the ball bouncing out once it hits the rim: the game fulfils all the law's requirements and is a real test of skill. This was not always thought to be the case with Hoop-la, popular since it was first introduced in 1909.

"The new game of hoop-la was in full swing, an expensive pastime for the patrons and profitable for the stall-holders," wrote the *Gazette* in 1909. "Twenty pennies were spent in a few minutes for one prize worth 2d." At one Fair, an inspector noted 165 hoops thrown in succession without a prize being won, and decided that this contravened the Betting Act. In another case in 1909, out of 252 throws only four were said to have been successfully aimed, though another fourteen hoops rolled back down the slope and landed on a prize by accident. Patrons did not realise the need to tilt the hoop when throwing it so that its angle matched that of the sloping stall. Some showmen were accused of putting prizes too close together, so that the hoop could not fall flat as required to win.

We still have rings to throw over stuffed toys, as we used to throw them over walking sticks; though at many of the stalls these days, children are given a consolation prize, such as a balloon, if they do not manage to ring an object.

Requiring a steady hand and a certain amount of luck are the machines in which a crane has to be manipulated to pick up toys embedded in Hundreds and Thousands: again, many childhood memories are of getting merely a handful of sweets as the slippery toys slid through the metallic jaws of the crane.

ROLLING

As well as hurling balls or weapons at targets, people were - and still are - asked to roll balls down or up a slope to fall into a hole or slot. Until the law intervened and insisted on tokens, pennies were rolled onto coloured squares: the coin had to clear the lines to win and mysteriously always seemed to collapse at the end of its run and straddle the line. "The pennies were large and the spaces small," was one rueful comment.

Today's youngsters are invited to try their skill at marble games, and skittles too have long been popular at Fairs.

DARTS

We have not been able to find many references to darts before 1930 but memories are fallible. In 1940 the Pinner Rotary Club set up a charity stall on one of the prime sites in Bridge Street, much to the chagrin of the showmen. They stuck their ground and enjoyed a great deal of custom as they invited visitors to the Fair to throw darts at pictures of German parachutists: if they speared an envelope they could keep its contents. In 1950, you could throw darts to "explode an atom bomb" by striking the right card: cards still appear at the Fair, sometimes looking a little worse for wear after a day at Hampstead. Again, there were rumours about the quality of the darts, no doubt spread by people who had not spent their youth in the saloon bar and whose eyes were not too straight.

What makes the darts competitions harder these days is the need sometimes to score less than a given number.

SHOOTING

Rifle-shooting has long been a favourite attraction for men: in 1885 it was thought to be "a more noble pastime" than the newly-devised coconut shies, and in 1886, you could shoot at eggs seated in the mouths of bottles. In 1904 the "Shooting Saloons" were "as well patronised as in recent years" though their constant noise was none too pleasurable. Clay pipes were the target.

Fair Enough?

Four years later, these saloons and "other aids to patriotism" were in abundance. Presumably as in 1941, the targets then represented perceived enemies of the country. They were usually placed outside Lines's shop in the High Street.

The only time the rifle galleries were not so well patronised was in 1940, when the fantasy world of the Fairground perhaps seemed too close to reality.

As with the darts, doubts have occasionally been expressed about the accuracy of the rifles and their sights and there are many accounts of by-standers being peppered with gun shot, but perhaps this was just inexperience (see page 84). "Most of the marksmen," said the reporter in 1885, "have never shot a rabbit in their lives." To help live out one's particular fantasy, the stalls were attractively labelled - "The Bisley Range" in 1910, or, rather more excitingly, "The Wells Fargo Express" in 1921, when you could ride shotgun with the Stagecoach.

In recent years, the rifle has become a cross-bow, and no doubt will soon be a laser-gun or other Star Trek weapon. On the other hand, in 1992 it was even possible to exercise one's skill at the mediaeval sport of archery at one of the stalls.

BOXING

The boxing booths mentioned by Torre appeared again in the poster of 1841 advertising the Fair and offering prizes for the "Art of Self-defence". These were bare-knuckle fights, which continued until the 1870's. Other Harrovians have written about illegal visits to the Fair, to try to win money in these booths. The professional pugilists, used to flooring unsuspecting yokels, were no doubt surprised to find opponents who had been taught to box in the school gymnasium.

Thomas Ellement remembered a time when the boxing booths were set up at a Fair in Harrow Recreation Ground during Winston Churchill's years at Harrow School (1888 - 92). The School's champion boxer took up the challenge and "gave the professional a thorough thrashing". The Fair was put out of bounds to the boys thereafter.

"An added interest," says the *Gazette* of 1908, "was provided by the boxing show, from the 'balcony' of which powerful specimens of manhood threw their challenges to all and sundry." These booths were usually to be found at the foot of Station Approach, by the old 'Victory'.

Boxing continued to be a major attraction at the Fair until the last war. Young men could always be found to try their luck: if they could survive a round or two with The Champion they could earn themselves £1, or later, £5. Ernie Parslow, a local resident, remembered as a youth being inveigled by the landlord of the Queen's Head to have a go. This worthy, the comically named Mr. J O King, had been Heavyweight Boxing Champion of Australia in his day. (When the Australian cricket team toured England in 1938, he flew the Australian flag outside his inn).

PINNER FAIR,

ON

Wednesday June 2nd, 1841,

A VARIETY OF

AMUSEMENTS,

Will be Displayed of different descriptions, at the above Fair, including the

ART

OF

Self Defence,

&c. &c.

The Prizes will consist of

Jackets, Caps, Hats, Slops, Trowsers, Waistcoats, &c.

TOO NUMEROUS TO MENTION

TO COMMENCE AT ONE O'CLOCK.

GREENE, PRINTER, STANMORE.

Above　　　Poster from 1841
Below left　The striker.
Below right Notice from a shooting saloon.

NO CROSS FIRING

Fair Enough?
STRONG MEN

Strong men (or women), who could perform impossible tasks with apparently heavy iron bars drew the impressionable crowds, as did escapologists: "The coils of rope with which they were fastened were to be loosed as if by magic by a series of wrigglings and painful contortions."

Another trick of the strong man was to lie down with a large stone on his stomach and invite spectators to break it with a sledge-hammer.

Less painful, except to the morale, was the Try Your Strength machine, known as The Striker. Early this century it usually appeared in photos at the foot of the High Street or by Chapel Lane, but more recently it found a pitch at the top of Bridge Street. All you had to do was to swing a mallet and strike a wooden peg: this sent an indicator smartly climbing up a vertical scale. Hit in the correct fashion, this could ring a bell at the top and sometimes win you a prize of a cigar or your money back. It was not always the strongest-looking men who managed this feat. This was presumably what was meant by the "thumping machine" mentioned in a report of 1881. Before the last war, the bell was said to be cracked and the mallet worn, and the Striker has now largely disappeared, along with other tests of personal prowess, designed to enable participants to impress onlookers.

SKILLS

Nowadays, it is nerve rather than strength that is tested on the various rides. There are still some stalls, though, where a steady hand is needed, like those devices seen at garden Fêtes in which a loop of wire has to be passed over another without making contact and setting off an alarm. One such is the stall where a coca-cola bottle has to be looped round the neck with a piece of string on the end of a stick and made to stand up. It is harder than it sounds. At the 1934 Fair, children were invited to the 'Magic Fishing Pond'. If they caught five fish they won a prize.

Modern boys have a variety of expensive electrical toys and some of these are beginning to find their way into fairgrounds, such as the radio-controlled cars that have to be guided round a circuit in 'Pit Stop'. Mechanical race games featuring horses were to be seen before the war in the 'Derby Race Game': in 1992 there was the 'Kentucky Derby'.

SHOWS

FREAKS

Henry Torre mentioned "shows" at the Fair in the 1830's and there have long been sideshows of a dubious kind to mystify or titillate a gullible public. Even in Shakespeare's day, the freak or "raree-show" was a principal attraction:

> "We'll have thee, as our rarer monsters are,
> Painted upon a pole, and underwrit,
> Here may you see the Tyrant."
>
> (*Macbeth* V.viii.25)

40

Mark Antony, enraged by Cleopatra, threatens to hand her over to Caesar for her to be hoisted up like a monster to be shown to fools. (*Antony & Cleopatra* IV.xii.36).

In *The Tempest*, Trinculo, the jester, finds the monster Caliban and at once sees the possibility of profit:

> "A strange fish ! Were I in England now, as once I was, and had but this fish painted, not a holiday fool there but would give a piece of silver: there would this monster make a man; any strange beast there makes a man; when they will not give a doit* to relieve a lame beggar, they will lay out ten to see a dead Indian."
>
> (II.ii.27)

(*: doit: a small coin)

("Painted" in two of these quotations refers to the painted sign or banners that advertised shows in the same way as an inn-sign).

Throughout the seventeenth and eighteenth centuries, people had been drawn by curiosity to stare at some malformed creatures. Some were thought to be mythical animals brought back by intrepid explorers, such as "mermaids" or "unicorns". A mermaid could well have been created by sewing a fish tail onto the skin of a monkey.

In Ben Jonson's *Bartholomew Fayre* (1614), one of the "devices" on show is a "bull with five legs and two pizzles." It had apparently been shown two years previously at Uxbridge Fair, so perhaps it had called in at Pinner, too.

Even human beings with some deformity were considered fair game: anyone extraordinarily thin, fat, tall or short would draw in the crowds and the Fat Lady at Pinner in 1929 was almost a stereotype. In 1814 it was the Fireproof Lady who was fashionable and a few years later the Pig-faced Lady made £150 for her owner at Bartholomew Fair in Smithfield. George Sanger has confessed how his Pig-faced Lady was created: she was in fact a small bear dressed in woman's clothing. Poked by a small boy hidden under a table, the bear would grunt apparently in answer to questions. She was the star turn at the Coronation Fair in Hyde Park in 1838.

He has also shown us the truth behind The Tallest Lady in the World: a girl of normal height with the aid of high heels, and a conveniently placed dais, all carefully concealed by long flowing draperies, gave an illusion that was quite impressive in a dimly-lit tent. Similarly the boy floating in air was not there because of ether, as advertised, but through the agency of a strong but thin metal framework that supported his apparently weightless condition.

One of his popular attractions was a shoal of trained fish fighting a naval battle: goldfish were induced to swim into a wire loop attached to a toy boat. As they swam around their tank, the ships would appear to be engaged in battle. Another of his shows was a Tame Oyster that Smoked a Pipe. For this, an oyster shell was mounted on a dark cloth on a table. Concealed pipes led from it to a boy again sitting below, who puffed smoke up the tube when required. At another Fair, in 1832, an "African savage" was really a bear dressed in a check suit.

Fair Enough?

In the nineteenth century, even the Royal Family were entertained by one of the most famous of these unusual characters, General Tom Thumb. Brought to England by Barnum, he gave his farewell performance at Uxbridge on St John the Baptist's Day, 1865. Really named Charles Stratton, he was three feet tall, and with his wife, infant daughter and a Miss Minnie Warren and a Commodore Nutt (whose carriage was a facsimile of a walnut shell) he performed songs and dances and gave an imitation of Napoleon. He made speeches and pretended to be a Grecian statue. The Commodore gave impersonations, performed military drill and played the drum and violin. All four adults weighed just over 100 lbs between them, being "the smallest human beings ever known". They were said not to be dwarfs but "blithe and merry little men and women in miniature". A child of four towered above them in height. (The Uxbridge Local History Library has a splendid poster giving these details).

An even smaller Tom Thumb was born in 1887: he was under two feet tall at the age of twenty. At the other extreme was Patrick O'Brien, the Irish Giant of 18th century fame, who was 8'7" tall at his peak, so to speak.

By 1901 tastes were beginning to change and the report on Pinner Fair, whilst deploring the unruly nature of the crowds, complained that "The attractions if they may be called so, were more numerous than before but there was no novelty. (They included) ...doubtful shows of extraordinary freaks."

Five years later, we were let into one of the secrets of the Fair.

Advertised as "the greatest freak of nature ever seen", a creature was said to be part seal, part alligator and part man. The reporter saw a young man in a booth wearing an overcoat over his shoulders and holding a cigarette in a right hand that was webbed like a duck. In front of some twelve spectators, he removed his coat and revealed a pink lady's vest. "Gentlemen", he said, "I am a freak. You see I have two swallows." He then revealed the cavernous formation of his throat. "Should there not," asked the reporter piously, "be a home for these unfortunates?" Modern sensitivities are obviously being formed here; though he does not appear to have been surprised at the peculiarities of the description given by the "barker" outside, nor to have wondered over the absence of both seals and alligators.

Sixty years ago, says Frances Brown, Sussex Fairs featured, not a Gorilla but a "Go-man-vu-la", a dried-up man. There too, was Tiny Tim, the descendant of Tom Thumb and only 28" high. Magee's Midgets visited Pinner in 1935, along with George Chadwick's Freaks. These included the Bearded Lady, the Lady Without a Middle and the Lobster-clawed Girl. In the 1970's there was a resurgence of interest in the freaks, with the Pig-faced Woman being resurrected along with the Cuban Two-headed Giant, the Two-headed Dwarf, and a variety of five-legged animals. There was the Spotted Lady Alive and the Lady in a Bottle.

Although the greasy poles had gone by 1939, "queer freaks, the like of which must have amazed the sturdy villagers of old, still (caused) London businessmen to gape with the same wonderment."

By the 1980's these aberrations or fakes had mostly disappeared from our Fair, and are now to be found only in the pages of a John Wyndham novel.

ANIMALS

As well as staring at deformed creatures, Fairground crowds have long been fascinated by seeing animals performing tricks. Though largely the preserve of the circus and in any case contrary to modern taste, many of these performing animals found their way into Fairs. Three hundred years ago, Ben Jonson mentioned a hare trained to play a drum. Then and later, horses like "Morocco" or "Clever Hans" made their name by signs of above-average intelligence in being apparently able to count or answer questions. "Learned pigs" or horses could, however, be trained quite easily to stop circling their trainer at the quiet click of a finger. If they pawed the ground they appeared to be pointing to a card or a number.

At Bartholomew Fair in 1775 a star attraction was a team of twelve canaries with toy muskets under their wings, which they 'fired' at each other.

More sinister was the Cave of Rats seen at Pinner in 1973. Sublimation of their fears possibly drew people to see rats crawling all over a woman in the booth. A two-year-old child was bitten by one when taken in by an older sister. Elsewhere in the last century showmen had shown a 'Kaffir' eating live rats in order to extract money from "Jugginses" wanting sensation. Nowadays, videos fulfil the same roles at home.

The previous year Pinner had been treated to the sight of monkeys in woolly bloomers. A brief allusion to the Fair in 1879 speaks of a "dog and monkey show" which appeared in the High Street and was "characterised as a nuisance."

Most animals, however, were to be seen in the travelling menageries like Wombwell's[7], one of which came to the Fair in 1911 and occupied Piercy's field off Paines Lane, on the site of what is now Paines Close. One old inhabitant recalls seeing a procession of elephants down the High Street on the evening before the Fair and many recall a circus tent in the fields beside Love Lane.

Sanger painted one of his elephants with whitewash and proclaimed "the only white elephant in captivity". When Wombwell's elephant died the latter countered by advertising "the only dead elephant in the Fair".

When Sanger's Circus came to Harrow in 1888 a star attraction was "Alpine Charlie" and his band of twelve ravenous wolves which had killed a horse a few months earlier. Sanger reveals that the horse was already dead when he himself let the wolves out of their cages. When attendants saw the wolves apparently devouring a horse they had just killed, they raised the alarm and panic ensued until the 'brave' trainer stepped in and led his actually docile animals back home. The alarming news, however, had spread rapidly as Sanger had hoped and people flocked in their thousands to see the ravenous monsters (see illustration on page 45).

*7 . Wombwell's Menagerie dominated the roads in the nineteenth century, inspiring admiration, envy and fear among the other showmen. Many pitched battles took place when the powerful Menagerie waggons were beaten to a favoured site by speedier stall-holders.

Fair Enough?

Another circus to tour the area was Fossett's, which was at the Swan and Bottle Field in Uxbridge in 1878 (see page 115).

At the other end of the scale, we might include the flea circus, the height (or depth?) of ingenuity. Fascinated audiences watched while diminutive creatures pulled loads far bigger than themselves or did incredible feats on a high wire. Jimmy Osborough brought his trained fleas to Pinner sixty years ago. .

If horses could be "trained" to count, humans could also deceive the eye. Bill Bright, a showman at the time of Queen Victoria's coronation, presented the Cackler Dance. A blindfolded girl danced rapidly between eggs placed on the floor, and even around a gentleman's gold watch borrowed from a member of the audience. No breakages occurred as the dancer could in fact see perfectly well where she put her nimble feet, but the suspense was electric. Some were quite harmless deceptions, like Professor Sands, whose "vacuum boots" allowed him to walk on the ceiling.

Dancing displays of various kinds could always be sure of luring in the men. The great Bartholomew Fair ran from 1133 to 1855, when it was stopped on the grounds of gross immorality. Men who visited some of the risqué shows have always been rather reluctant to commit to paper what they were perhaps conned into seeing.

Possibly they were ashamed to admit that they had been attracted, or it was merely that they wanted to enjoy the sight of others being tricked as they had been? The immodest Nautch Girls could be seen for a penny at the top of Bridge Street in 1908. One elderly gentleman remembers being puzzled as a boy by seeing hula-hula dancers in grass skirts, advertising their stall, offering inducements to unimaginable sights inside the booth. In the 1960's titles like "The Abode of Love and Laughter" or "the Space of Love" can be seen in photographs of Pinner Fair, and there are coy references in reports to "girlie shows." In 1959 the Council were worried by rumours of a nude display in one of the strip-tease tents. We await confirmation of these rumours from adults who attended, but most showmen are concerned for their reputation and would be unlikely to allow any immorality.

That the "raree show" was formerly the mainstay of Pinner Fair can be seen by a report in 1881: "It was the cause of much thankfulness this year to find but one show. In former years there have been many, and few can doubt the demoralising influence they had upon the public."

Alongside some of the most "demoralising" of these shows can be found from time to time members of some religious organisation battling against the sins around them. One such was established in Bridge Street in the 1960's, run by the Watford City and Village Gospel Team. Announcing that The Wicked Shall be Turned into Hell, they certainly commanded admiration for their courage.

44

LORD GEORGE SANGER'S
WORLD-FAMED
ENGLISH & CONTINENTAL CIRCUS.

Second Visit to the Provinces for 13 Years.

N.B.—The Public must not be deceived by any Circus they have previously seen, as this is the only complete Circus and Hippodrome that has visited England for at least the last Century.

MR. ATKINS' FIELD, HARROW,
TUESDAY, SEPTEMBER 18th ;
WATFORD, SEPTEMBER 19TH.

All the Sports and daring of ANCIENT ROME.
The Gladiators, by Fifty Skilled Artistes.
EXCITING KANGAROO HUNT.
Introducing Australian Life, by Six Real Kangaroos and Natives in True Costumes.
ALPINE CHARLIE.
His Wonderful Kennel of 12 Ravenous Wolves. The Great Fight between Man and Wolves, and the Defeat. Alpine Charlie will feed the ravenous Monsters from his Naked Hand. These are the Wolves that attacked and killed the horse at Lord George Sanger's Amphitheatre on Saturday, February 11th, 1888.

The Grand Historical Spectacular Pageant,
ST. GEORGE AND THE FIERY DRAGON.
THE GREAT OSTRICH HUNT,
With Real Ostriches, Dogs and Natives in true Costumes.
Salamander War Horse and Fire Kings.

LORD GEORGE SANGER'S
BUFFALO BILL AND HIS COWBOYS.
Scenes of Western Border Life in America, by Indians, Cowboys, and Scouts.
THE BEST CLOWNS
That have ever appeared before the Public.
THE GRAND WATERPROOF PAVILION.
The whole of the seats (6d. excepted) are wholly carpeted, and free from draughts.
Be sure and see the Grand Procession—Novel, Gorgeous, and Original—at One o'clock, rain or fine.

Admission: 3s., 2s., 1s., and 6d.

God save the Queen.

Advertisement for Sanger's Circus at Harrow, 1888.

45

ACTING

There were other sideshows, too, of greater appeal to the family and involving some form of theatrical entertainment.

Since Elizabethan days at least, travelling players had visited the larger Fairs, some of the companies like Middleton's becoming famous. In 1604 they had been banned, along with bear-baiting and the nine men's morris. The players often included such characters as Harlequin and Columbine, Pantaloon and the Saracen, or assorted clowns, demons, gladiators or Crusaders. Frequently, the words were extemporised and costumes remained unchanged, whatever the play. Dickens has described such a touring company, with the audience standing in the darkened tent to watch a melodrama like "Maria Marten" or "The Story of Bluebeard".

When Greenwich Fair closed in 1857, Johnson and Lee's theatrical show moved on to Uxbridge Fair: it is possible that they entertained Pinner audiences also.

Ten years later, when Pinder's Circus visited Harrow, the highlight was to be a dramatic tableau portraying the Battle of Bosworth ("My Kingdom for a horse!") with the "slain steed being carried from the battlefield in a procession of knights and dames." Unfortunately, heavy rain forced the performance to be cancelled.

Two hundred years ago, there would have been peep-shows, early ancestors of the "What the Butler Saw" machines of seaside piers. Lit by smoking candles and operated by strings, cut-out figures would move jerkily to animate a reconstruction of some dramatic event. Great battles of the Napoleonic Wars, or, later of the Crimea, were portrayed with a liberal amount of simulated gore. Trafalgar and the Charge of the Light Brigade were particular favourites. The assassination of Abraham Lincoln or the funeral of the Duke of Wellington likewise appealed to morbid human nature. A national horror story, such as a riot or massacre, would be translated into graphic scenes viewed through the peep-show glass. One can now only guess at what was shown in "The Terrors of Limehouse" shown at Pinner in 1934.

Since the Middle Ages, puppet shows had been popular: Ben Jonson has one at the climax of his play, in which the puppets present a modernised, cockney version of Hero and Leander, with the destruction of Sodom and Gomorrah and the discovery of the Gunpowder Plot somehow woven into the story. Punch and Judy became the most persistent of the puppets. Some were due to come to Pinner in 1910, advertised as a topical suffragette Punch and Judy; but they failed to materialise and the paper wondered whether they had failed to pay their dues or whether someone had "queered their pitch". In 1952 a large crowd gathered in the High Street to watch Press and Kitlee's Punch and Judy show.

CINEMA

The flickering candles and pulled strings of the peep-show gave way gradually to new inventions, each with ever more exotic names as the twentieth century approached. In 1869 the Zoetrope had scenes painted on a cylinder. When viewed through slits, as the cylinder turned the pictures appeared to move. Edison produced the Kinetoscope in 1887 for touring Fairs, its pictures being normal Fairground attractions like performing animals and strong men.

The Phantoscope of 1894 was a modified kaleidoscope, and in 1910, in the field alongside Pinner Church, the Bioscope was unveiled as "an invention of great interest to many". Sharing the field the following year with the menagerie, it was described as "living picture entertainment". At last the cinematograph had arrived. About fifty people could be crammed into a tent to watch a flickering film, often interrupted by mechanical failures, with the roaring of the nearby animals acting as sound effects. The Bioscope did not last for long, however, as permanent cinemas were being built and the novelty wore off. Already, by 1907, the Gaumont Company of Piccadilly had been advertising its latest novelty, the Chronophone, which showed pictures with sound accompaniment. Now, ironically, the cinemas themselves are closing and turning to that mainstay of the Fairground - Bingo.

Part of the fun of these "shows" of course has always been to listen to the "Barker", the man with a fine line in patter, whose drum and trumpets would attract the crowds to listen to his tales. "After a long tale of wonderful exploits has been unfolded, the speech interspersed with the melodic sounds of a huge wooden rattle, the admiring crowd fills the improvised hall and the performance begins."

Derek Trotter of "Only Fools and Horses" has many ancestors.

GAMBLING

Wherever large crowds gather, there are pickings to be had, and all Fairs were adorned by the card-sharp or some other confidence trickster, asking punters to Find the Lady. Paul Daniels has done much to uncover the tricks of the trade perpetrated on unsuspecting customers. The authorities have tried to ensure that there was an element of skill involved in all the stalls inviting you to Try Your Luck, though Tombola still survives on charity stalls.

At Harrow Fair in 1864, Richard Tarling, aged 17, was given 14 days' hard labour for having a brass rod on a spindle turning over a coloured cloth and asking customers to bet on certain numbers painted on the cloth, a device called The Spinner. Later versions, with flashing lights and pictures of film stars or sports personalities appeared at Pinner Fair with apparent impunity. Recently, too, you could pick a lucky straw containing a numbered ticket entitling you to a prize. Bingo has even clickety-clicked at times here. Sometimes perishable goods are offered as prizes to prove that winning numbers do in fact exist.

At race courses in particular, but also no doubt at Pinner Fair, "tag tables" were all the rage. After betting on a number, punters threw a box of a dozen dice. Rapid mathematical calculations of the total by the stall-holder would somehow always end in a number without a stake, unless there was a stooge in the audience, whose success was rewarded in shiny new coins to attract still more patients for a little deft financial surgery.

47

Above   A "pitcher" at work before the last war with china bargains (photo - Mr Bentley).

Below   A fortune-teller sets up her stall in front of the partly demolished Parish Hall in 1966

The desire to gamble finds an outlet in the Amusement Arcades, with their fruit and pin-ball machines, though local bye-laws often banned these. Slot machines were sometimes relegated to fortune telling, ball games and "What the Butler Saw".

Three Arcades were seen at Pinner in 1966, and up by Safeway's in 1992 were Sassy Sally's Casino and the Silver Dollar, replete with computer games waiting to tempt Nintending customers. Asked about his visit to the Fair, one ten-year-old replied, "I didn't go in any Arcades. For one, I'm not good at any computer games; for two I don't waste money; and for three, what's the point?"

Perhaps there is hope for the world after all.

FORTUNE TELLING

While the young try their luck on the slot machines, others want to know what the future has in store for them. The clairvoyants and "Society" palmists have a field-day. In 1908 there were thought-readers, phrenologists reading bumps, physiognomists telling your fortune from your face, and "Fortune tellers dotted here and there giving out their sage and wondrous mind-power to the obvious amazement of onlookers."

No fewer than seventeen palmists graced Pinner Fair in 1935, including seven Gipsy Lees. In 1992 caravans were occupied by Gipsy Rose Lee, Gipsy Rosa Lee, Gipsy Betsy Lee and Romany Gipsy Lee. They were too busy having their palms crossed with silver to be asked if they were in fact all related, though the grandmother of at least one of them is known to have been at her stall at the top of the High Street in the 1920's when it cost three old pence to have your palm read and 1/- (5p) for the crystal ball. There were long queues for fortune tellers in 1976.

Katherine Mansfield describes a masculine version at a Bank Holiday Fair:

"Under a tree, Professor Leonard, in cap and gown, stands beside his banner. He is here "for one day," from the London, Paris and Brussels Exhibition, to tell your fortune from your face. And he stands, smiling encouragement, like a clumsy dentist. When the big men, romping and swearing a moment before, hand across their sixpence, and stand before him, they are suddenly serious, dumb, timid, almost blushing as the Professor's quick hand notches the printed card. They are like little children caught playing in a forbidden garden by the owner, stepping from behind a tree."

STALLS

As the main purpose of the Fair originally was the sale of goods, stalls have always formed a major part of the day, though these have diminished in number since the growth of shops. Ben Jonson, writing in 1614, has showmen selling hobby-horses, puppets, dolls (then called "babies"), rattles, drums, fiddles, ballads, mousetraps, tinderboxes, Toby dogs, purses, pouches, pin-cases, pipes, jews' harps, whistling birds, halberts, painted ladies (were these some early form of pin-ups?) and horses. The latter were traded by horse-coursers, renowned for their trickery - hence the need to look horses in the mouth before buying, and similarly with pigs in pokes.

Fair Enough?

Over the past two hundred years at Pinner many a tawdry[8] item has doubtless been sold, from a new tea set to jewellery and false teeth. Hawkers originally sold ornaments, earthenware, mats and mirrors. Today, occasional itinerant sellers offer sun-glasses, Mexican jumping-beans or gas-filled balloons, some for charity. In 1911 photographers were able to take instant circular pictures with a kind of early Polaroid camera that printed photographs on the spot for 3d each. Nowadays the genuine market stall "pitcher" with his renowned patter is rarely seen ("I'm not asking ten pounds for this canteen, nor eight pounds but only a fiver.")

Ben Jonson explains the worth of these merchandising stalls:

> "The wares are the wares of devils and the whole Fair is the shop of Satan! They are hooks and baits, very baits, that are hung out on every side, to catch you, and to hold you, as it were, by the gills and by the nostrils, as the fisher doth."

Mind you, those words were spoken by Zeal-of-the-Land Busy, a zealous Puritan and spoil-sport. Doubtless his kind never came to disturb the pleasures of Pinner Fair.

If you felt you had succumbed unduly to the wares of Satan and had eaten too much candy-floss, you could check for damage on the scales placed ready - as in 1908 - at the foot of the High Street, to Try Your Weight, rather than your strength. The stallholder here would guess your weight and you only paid if he was right. Thin, big-boned people were more successful at deceiving him than others.

CHILDREN

The Fair is nowadays very much the preserve of the young, certainly of the young-in-heart. The youngest come in the morning or early afternoon for a little gentle fun before the crowds become too thick. They can bounce around on the Undulating Moon Walk or Bouncy Castle; they can become confused in the Chinese Mirror Maze (and who cannot recall the distorting mirrors on the piers of yesteryear?) or they can have fun in the Rio Madness Fun House.

Here, steps slide up and down, floors move from side to side and keeping one's feet is a problem. The clever ones quickly discover that if you walk up one set of steps it is easier than having feet planted on stairs moving in opposite directions, which tends to encourage the splits. Blasts of air add to the surprises, and the children are dumped unceremoniously down a steep slide at the end. "You get spooked in the dark by Frankenstein when he pops out from nowhere. This happens in the Ghost House as well." The Ghost Train or Haunted House has for long been on hand for those whose tastes lie in being frightened, but who draw the line at live rats. One of the Haunted Houses was called Frankenstein's Castle.

8   Tawdry: Addison, in *English Fairs and Markets*, p. 21, explains that the word derives from St Etheldreda, a seventh century abbess in Ely, known locally as St Audrey. She rescued a penitent thief, whose chains were struck off, and he became a monk, hanging his chains in the abbey. These were reproduced in lace and sold at Ely Fair until 1913 as "St Audrey's chains". Through time, the name was corrupted to "tawdry" and applied to any kind of cheap or pretentious adornment. The OED says, on the other hand, that St Audrey thought she had been punished for wearing rich necklaces of jewels. She was a most revered saint and it was to cater for the many pilgrims to Ely Cathedral that Ely Fair probably grew up (see page 106).

A recent young visitor recalled:

"The Ghost House was very scary. The first door swung open, revealing a skeleton. I screamed. Then I walked on the moving floor. I managed to get across it and found myself in front of a door which said 'Witches' Dump.' Do you dare? I thought. I pushed the door open and found myself in a load of rubbish. When I finally clambered over it and got to the end, I found that either I got bumped on the head with a hammer or else got sprayed. You can guess what happened to me. The water pattered on my head and shoulders. When I came out my mother wondered how I had got wet. Little did she know."

Little did Mother know, too, of other reasons for young men visiting the haunted House:

"This was the best event of all, for nasty boys would wait until a group of girls went in and follow them in to the pitch dark corridors of the tent. The female squeals were certainly not caused by the cold blasts of air that shot up from openings in the floor. Nor was the cause the moving floor or the fluorescent skeletons and skulls!"

A skeleton outside draws your attention and the screams from inside persuade you that it is fun. Again, perhaps it is better to face up to fears with your best friend beside you than have private nightmares. The workings of the human mind are strange. So too are the demands of the human body.

RIDES

ROUNDABOUTS

All of us, it seems, have an urge to defy gravity, to spin round faster than the earth on which we are already spinning, to travel at frightening speeds upside down and round.

Earlier, we referred to the Circus and Menagerie that came to Pinner in 1911. Another kind of Circus visited us in 1898. Driven by steam and lit by electricity, it was certainly an attraction, enjoying "the largest patronage". It was a kind of roundabout, one for small children. It can be seen labelled "Circus" in a photograph of the Fair in 1908. Frances Brown speaks of "Harris's Steam Riding Circus", invented by William Sanger, the circus proprietor. This kind of ride is still in great demand, especially on the mornings of Fair day.

Nowadays the youngest children can sit in a little train completing a turning circle that many motorists would envy. For many years this has been seen at the foot of the High Street; recently it has been joined by many other merry-go-rounds with insects, tea-cups, police motor cycles or animals in or on which to ride. Each does a slow and solemn circle, to the evident delight of all concerned. Dizziness is apparently only a figment of adult imagination.

Primitive roundabouts for children can be seen in 17th century pictures from Asia: these take the form of a horizontal cart wheel, to which are fixed seats for children. Later, crude shapes representing horses were used, to let people imagine they were

51

Fair Enough?

really on horseback. The first horse roundabouts, called "Dobbies", had rigid horses that simply acted as seats, but these were then pivoted, making the legs move independently to imitate the action of a horse in motion. Later designers, by an ingenious arrangement of cranks or wheels, could make the horses move up and down, and the rider could enjoy the experience of horse-riding without its expense.

Moved at first by hand (often by ponies or even small boys in exchange for a free ride) they were adapted to steam-driven engines by 1865, and became the central attractions at any Fair.

Henry Torre mentioned the roundabouts in the 1830s and it is difficult to imagine Pinner Fair without them, though recent newspaper reports do hint that with the advent of monster machines the old fashioned ones may be nearing their economic end.

"The carousel is the prettiest of all rides," said one little girl recently. "The music is sweet and I like how you can see it playing."

"My favourite ride," said another, "is on the lovely old carousel. It is very expensive, but we have always gone on it so we like to keep up the tradition. I try to find a white horse, because I think it is really pretty."

The carousel is derived from an old Moorish sport that was adapted by 18th century horsemen as a riding exercise, of the sort now seen only at tattoos or the Royal Tournament, in which the riders perform manoeuvres while riding in a circle. The word was then used for a roundabout, particularly in the United States.

The horses were beautifully carved, many by craftsmen from Savage's of King's Lynn or Anderson's of Bristol, and each was named either after a famous race-horse or perhaps a member of the showman's family. For many, the sight of these proud and rather intimidating beasts, resplendent in their Moorish or Byzantine paintwork, represents all the joy and splendour and escapism of the Fairground, and is one of childhood's most abiding memories. The Gallopers were the King of the Fair.

By 1890, Savage's were producing roundabouts with four horses abreast, providing rides for up to 56 people at a time.

A much earlier variety of roundabout was the Velocipede. When cycling became the rage in the last century, Savage's produced a machine on which riders sat on bicycles, their pedalling being the only motive power - the faster they worked their legs, the faster the roundabout circled. Experienced travellers merely freewheeled, letting others do the work. They even had a steam-driven version, one of which was bought by Thomas Pettigrove in 1870.

This family of Pettigrove has been coming to Pinner for well over a century. They were already regarded as regular visitors in 1883, and in 1885 are to be seen in a picture of the Fair with their "Great London Roundabouts". Their present set of Golden Gallopers was built by Tidman's of Norwich; as well as horses this has a gondola and two splendid dragon chariots, which were to be seen at the Wembley Exhibition in 1924.

Above   A detail from the photo on page 35 showing London Roundabouts.
Below   Bridge Street in 1908 with the striker, roundabouts and swings.
The building on the corner of Love Lane had only just been built;
next to Harris, the wine merchant, Sterman, the bootmaker, and
Fyfe, who sold art needlework, the remaining shops are empty.

Drawing by David Muriss.

On the same site each year, the most difficult they occupy at any Fair, because of the slope, they dominate the High Street from their eminence by the Church.

Almost as fascinating as sitting astride the magnificent beasts and lording it over the spectators is the scene when these devices are being set up. The road is marked out beforehand in yellow. The centre beams comprising the gantry are carefully stationed and levelled. Lorries uncouple trailers and reverse onto others, and the centre truck is carefully backed into place. This contains the gearing to operate the ride. Then the organ is positioned and covered with its gaily painted panels. The wooden spokes forming the roof, called "swifts", are fixed in place, and covered with the awning, or tilt. Round the edge of this are the sounding boards like a pelmet, on which the artist has painted in ornate script "Grand Golden Galloping Horses". The steps are added and all is ready - just in time for a drink before the pubs shut. The lads have earned their reward. The setting up in 1992 was enlivened by the youngest member of the family who must have been at least three, carrying a beam as tall as himself.

In the 1960's, local men helped with the job, Herbert Parslow being made an honorary member of the Showmen's Guild for his work.

Carter's, the showmen of Maidenhead, have a similar Tidman's carousel, built in about 1895 and driven by an equally ancient engine called "Anna". The ride is decorated with pictures of Edwardian music-hall stars and turns to the music of a 46-key Gavioli organ, built in Paris in 1900. This carousel still visits Fairs in the locality.

Pettigrove's organ is even bigger, the 89-key Black Forest Gavioli mechanical organ. For all of us, its sound is nostalgic, romantic, exciting and the epitome of all that is meant by Going to the Fair.

At the Pinner Fire Brigade Fête on Whit Monday, 1898, in a field in West End Lane, the Grand Old English Carnival included such attractions as Bird's Royal Mammoth Steam Galloping Horses, and the New Orchestrion presented by Imhoff of London. It seems a reasonable assumption that they would have stayed on for the Fair two days later.

In 1904, another roundabout on a more level site occupied the centre of Bridge Street at the end of Chapel Lane:

> "The gigantic roundabout, resplendent in its gold and red-bedecked centre, and driven by a large and powerful traction engine, accounted for a great deal of space."

Before the last war, this was run by Fred Gray. It was just such a large traction engine that in 1919 ran down the High Street out of control (see page 82).

Steam-driven organs were introduced by 1880, and were changed to electric working after 1945. Their music is provided by "books" of folded sheet music with punched holes, like the old pianola, that are driven through the key-frame by a small variable-speed motor. Another electric motor drives a centrifugal blower to provide the wind to sound the pipes and work the drums, cymbals, xylophone or triangle.

Fair Enough?

There is usually a fairly dated repertoire of music-hall or popular songs, like *The Blue Danube*, *Pack Up Your Troubles*, *Annie Laurie* or *Lady of Spain*. In 1923, the organs played "unclassical but ever popular songs like *Caravan* or *I Want Some Money*, both peculiarly appropriate to the occasion." It mattered little as long as it was jolly, recognisable, blatant and (yes) raucous.

These organs were splendid creations, by inventors like Gavioli or his assistant, Marenghi. In 1909 one could cost as much as £9000 though the average was £2000. These lords of the Fairground should not be demeaned by being referred to as "hurdy-gurdies", which were strictly speaking small hand instruments in which the strings were struck by a hand-turned wheel. (The name was later applied popularly to the barrel-organ, familiar in Victorian street scenes with its attendant monkey.)

Let the reporter of 1885 set the scene for us:

> "From a quiet peaceful retreat, Pinner changed into a scene of the wildest noise and tumult on Wednesday last, when the annual Fair was held. In the 'good old days', Fairs, we may suppose, were of a very different description to that which has just taken place in our neighbouring hamlet.

> Then, music and dancing were the staple elements of enjoyment; the lads and lasses met on the green and enjoyed the healthful recreation of the dance in a clear and untainted atmosphere, and revelled in innocent mirth.

> But very different is the picture of the 19th century Fair. The Arcadian simplicity of former days has given place to a state of things almost revolting in its contrast. The steam roundabout with its screaming engine and blatant barrel-organ replete with music-hall tunes, the noise of the guns at the shooting galleries, the ear-splitting cries of the coconut men, the shouts of a hundred stall-keepers, and the roar of the traffic together make such a deafening hubbub that the wonder is such a coarse entertainment is countenanced by an enlightened public."

Some organs were replaced by the Panatrope in 1926, an early form of amplified record-player. Nowadays, the carousel organ has to compete, not only with neighbouring church bells, but with daunting decibels, mind-numbingly rapped out from ghetto-blasting, heavily metallic, low-fidelity amplifiers urgently broadcasting the rhythms of the new age (see page 85).

Sometimes, the roundabout horses were replaced by cockerels, ostriches or even flying pigs. These rides then had names like "Poultry Farm" or "Giant Bantams". For those who wanted a more demure ride, gondolas or chariots were provided, so that ladies could sit in modesty and even small children could be accommodated. The gondolas were often decorated with florid pictures of mermaids.

One variety, patented in 1880, had sailing ships instead of gondolas, the machinery imitating cleverly the pitching and tossing of a yacht at sea. Once again, patrons could experience thrills beyond their normal horizons. This "Sea-on-Land" machine became very popular and toured the country from 1881, though an earlier primitive version had been seen at Greenwich as early as 1835.

One ingenious designer had balloons in which to ride, which turned on their own axis as the roundabout revolved, thus anticipating the later developments of machines like the Waltzer.

Railway carriages were used, too, to attract rustics who had little opportunity of riding on the real thing: showmen have always been ready to pander to people's fanciful dreams. But with the coming of the Metropolitan Railway to Pinner in 1885, people were demanding even greater thrills, and planes were used to simulate flying. When everyone flew, the planes were replaced by rocket ships and moon buggies.

SCENIC RAILWAYS

The railway trains did not pitch and toss like ships or horses. Instead, they were made to climb up and down artificial hills and valleys as they circled, and the switchback or scenic railway was born. First seen at Pinner in 1910, this was so called because the centre driving machinery was hidden by elaborate painted scenery, so that you could imagine you were travelling through the countryside. One model even had another train running in a contrary direction inside the turning circle, to give a greater impression of speed. Electric motors underneath each carriage meant that the centre space could be devoted to even more spectacular scenic devices, with fountains or waterfalls. The extra weight these needed, however, made them short-lived.

The earlier simple name of "Ups and Downs" gave way to more sophisticated forms like "Mont Blanc", "Airways", "The Matterhorn", "Moon Rocket" or "Space Ships". "The Caterpillar" was a particular favourite with courting couples, as when it gathered speed, a hood covered the cars and left the riders in the dark. When the cars were changed to animals and adapted for younger children, the rides were known collectively as "Noah's Arks". For teenagers, the "Alpine Express", seen by Woolworth's in 1992, travels up and down while circling at terrifying speed. "It makes me sick just to look at it," said one youngster.

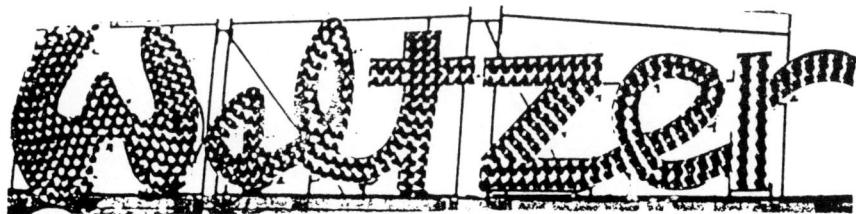

The Big Wheel at dusk (Photo JG).

WHEELS

There are a number of rides that involve sitting in a chair and being flung round. The more staid of these are the wheels. Like the famous one in Vienna, the Big Wheel towers over Bridge Street by the railway bridge and from the top you can see every inch of the Fair - provided, that is, that you have not closed your eyes in fear at the swift descent. In 1975, it was alongside Woolworth's in Bridge Street; by 1983 it had sidled across the road to stand outside the Red Lion Parade.

Although a primitive diamond-shaped wheel appeared at a Fair in 1832, the first mechanical one was seen at the Great Exhibition in 1851. Braithwaite[9] describes a big wheel at the Earls Court Exhibition of 1894: it was 280 feet in diameter and held 1200 people at a time in forty carriages. Even Pinner Fair could not cope with that one. Carter's Steam Fair are still travelling with an original Ferris Wheel.

Later versions were called Sky Wheel or Flying Saucer. The Chair Lift, or Chair-o-Plane, first introduced about 1922, flings the seats out at right angles as the speed increases and gives a better sensation of flying. The Super Trooper is comparatively demure and decorative. Couples sit under umbrellas or 'parachutes' as the wheel revolves vertically. The Rockoplane in the High Street made bystanders gasp in 1992 as it swung people up, down and around with abandon, and disgorged them shaken and indeed stirred.

If that is too tame for you, there is the Voyager, where you sit in a time capsule to be flung up and down at speed whilst turning upside down and reversing direction alarmingly. This is presumably descended from the Dive Bomber invented by Lee Eyerly of the USA in 1938. Braithwaite describes the action:

> "Two revolving cabins were pivoted at the ends of independently rotating arms. Capable of either looping the loop or being checked in mid-flight and suddenly reversed, the ride was nothing if not exciting. But with a (maximum) of eight paying passengers and a complexity of highly-stressed moving parts, profitable operation was difficult to achieve."

Those anxious for the safety of travellers aboard The Voyager will be relieved to know that, once inside the capsule, riders are fitted with shoulder restraints and a foam-rubber lap pad. The machine cannot operate until all the safety devices are in place and the door firmly closed.

More and more ingenuity has been expended by the showmen in applying new technology to make rides even more thrilling and apparently dangerous. Riders can be pivoted in small circles as they revolve round the main axis, as in Savage's Razzle Dazzle of 1893, or in its later manifestations as the Japanese Airship or the Whirligig. These became the Waltzer, the Octopus, the Satellite or the Meteorite as the pivoting arms rose from the horizontal and explored further permutations of dizziness. Certainly there is no shortage of new names, as the Waltzer is succeeded by the Sizzler, Orbiter, Skydiver or Asteroids in new versions of planetary motion.

9 *Fairground Architecture 1968*

Fair Enough?

The centrifugal cage - the Rotorcage, seen at Pinner as early as 1961 - in which victims are pinned against the sides as the cage whizzes round eccentrically seems to be the ultimate in masochistic pleasure: but no doubt something even more fiendish is on its way.

In the 1950's, some rides like the Vampire Jets had individual joysticks to allow riders, by means of compressed air, to control the extent of their aerial turmoil.

The truly terrifying rides now possible on permanent sites like Margate, Alton Towers, Thorpe Park or Euro Disney have bred a race of youngsters with apparently cast-iron stomachs and nerves of steel. The sense of danger, the thrill of speed, and the changing of one's equilibrium are all reasons for the popularity of these rides among people ever in search of new sensations to brighten routine lives. "I enjoy being frightened," explained one teenager as she stumbled off The Voyager.

These permanent sites can build larger rides, perhaps involving a water splash, but the Roller Coaster of the seaside holiday camp has found new life at Pinner as the Rollaghosta: it has carriages that pass through a haunted house. Michael Ware illustrates a compact portable version of the Big Dipper, known as the Figure of Eight, but even this would be too big for Pinner.

Of recent design are the Miami Surf Rides, in which passengers sit in a long horizontal row of chairs that revolve vertically while the riders at least remain the right way up. Screams of joy emanate from these, fearsome though they may seem to the timid or elderly as the chairs suddenly change direction and accelerate rapidly.

Modern showmen offer "white-knuckle" rides, hair-raising opportunities that subject the body to the strains and G-forces normally experienced only by test pilots. No wonder a notice at Pinner Fair recently announced, "RUMBUSTIOUS RIDE: NOT FOR WIMPS."

A brief period of popularity before the first war was enjoyed by the Joy Wheel. Built for the pleasure of spectators as much as for the participants, this consisted of a domed disc on which people sat and tried to remain as it span ever faster and they were flung off in undignified fashion. Collins's largest could hold seventy people in 1911, with seating for a thousand round the outside. A smaller version called a Devil's Disc and a more complex version known as the Witching Wheel did not survive the war. A more violent form was the Wiggle Waggle, in which riders ended up in a heap on the floor.

SWINGS

A visit to any children's recreation ground will show their eternal delight in swinging to and fro or flying at speed down the slides. 'Rock' and 'Swing' had other meanings in a quieter age. Along with the various kinds of roundabout, the swings have been one of the most popular attractions of the fairground since the 17th century. Both were equally popular with the showmen, who traditionally would use the gains on one to make up for losses on the other, though there was some rivalry at times between men who only had one or the other: the roundabouts could carry 36 or more, but the swing could only take two or four at a time and it took longer to load.

The space occupied by swings means that their owners must pay a large rental for their pitch. Economic forces mean that with only a relatively few riders, the swings are too costly to run, and they now no longer come to Pinner Fair, where costs per foot run are comparatively expensive.

Yet the swing-boats were very satisfying. Torre remembered them from the 1830s, and they were still attending Pinner Fair in the 1980s. Originally up by what is now Grange Gardens, they were latterly to be found by the Red Lion or the Marsh Road railway bridge. It was good to be able to make the boats swing by your own efforts, instead of being mechanically or electrically propelled. There was something satisfying, too, about the velvet ropes that swathed the chains from which they swung, and many a pensioner recalls the texture and the pleasure to this day. We hope the carousel will not follow the swings into oblivion.

The dubious report of 1881, apparently recording a Saturday Fair in July, speaks of "steam roundabouts accompanied by the usual parasites in the shape of swings and shooting galleries." Devotees will take great exception.

As technology advanced, a new steam-driven swing-boat arrived. Called the steam yacht, it could hold several people at once and gave a realistic feeling of being in a yacht at sea. A 1920 photograph shows Harry Gray setting up his steam yachts in Bridge Place, around the traction engine that provided the motive power.

There are believed to be only two of these yachts still in action. One, built in 1921 by Savage's of King's Lynn, has its original boat, Columbia, still swinging, though its partner, Shamrock, named after Sir Thomas Lipton's America Cup yacht, has been renamed Britannia. The amusement caterers, Carter's have refurbished them, along with the 1901 Savage engine, Yorky, and a new organ by Michael Dean. They were the highlights of a Steam Fair at Rickmansworth in August 1992.

DODGEMS

Part of the attraction of a Fairground is being able to do things that are normally forbidden or that are too dangerous, like crashing your car deliberately into someone else's. The Dodgems allowed frustrated road-hogs to bump away to their heart's content. Invented in the 1920 s, they appeared at the Wembley Empire Exhibition in 1924 and were introduced to Fairs along the south coast by 1933. Howard Spring, writing in 1943, remembered pre-war Fairs at Pinner with "electric floors on which motor cars would crash and swerve." Many of these were made by Lang Wheels of Hillingdon Heath, who supplied "De-Luxe Bumper Cars with an all-steel streamlined body and deeply cushioned upholstery." Some Dodgem tracks allowed movement in any direction and head-on crashes were the norm, with attendant snarl-ups and snarling attendants. Others were more organised and the cars travelled demurely around a track all going in the same general direction.

Earlier versions had used petrol driven cars, but these often proved to be unreliable. In 1950, the "bumper cars" were said to be rare visitors to Pinner though Tom Smith brought them again in 1952, but in the 1970 s and 1980 s they were well patronised

Fair Enough?

at their site near the entrance to Love Lane. They no longer appear here, though they were to be seen recently at the Rickmansworth Steam Fair, decorated with rock stars of yesteryear.

Popular at Ruislip in the 1930s was the Wall of Death, in which spectators watched experts risking their necks driving motor-cycles round a vertical wall. Strictly a spectator-sport, one version had lions sitting on the sidecar or riding pillion. At other Fairs, and possibly therefore at Pinner too, have been seen rides like the Brooklyn Cake Walk and the Electric Jumpers. The moving platforms that made people dance involuntarily in the former are now to be seen in the children's Fun House. Pinner, though, was not particularly innovative: a glance at the list of attractions in 1935 (see page 72) shows only one "modern" ride, the Mono Rail.

HELTER-SKELTER

In our glimpse at a children's recreation ground, we mentioned the slide as one of the perennial attractions. Its adoption by showmen seems to have been long delayed. The helter-skelter was first introduced in 1906 when Walker's of Tewkesbury advertised "Portable helter-skelter lighthouses". It appears to have avoided Pinner until 1932, when a new delight arrived, called Slipping the Slip. At the top of the High Street, near the swing-boat site, you could sit on a mat and slide down the outside of a tower built like a lighthouse that dwarfed the nearby houses. It soon became a favourite with children, who could not resist having repeat rides.

Passengers slide down sitting on a coconut mat; if they outstrip it in their haste, they come to know the meaning of the term "hot seat", and friction burns have to be treated. Part of the pleasure of the slide is the chance offered to spectators to enjoy seeing others collapsing at the bottom in undignified positions.

Its site varied over the years, but its great height made it easy to be seen in photographs of the Fair. A famous photo by A W Kerr, taken in 1950 and published in *Good Housekeeping* and *The Villager*, shows it by Church Farm. Another one was placed at the top of Bridge Street and was said to deposit its load of children practically into the police station. After the war, it moved down nearer the Dodgems outside the Red Lion and its lights were an added attraction at night. The one in the High Street was not seen there after 1955. Modern ones, in Marsh Road and Bridge Street, circle round a more functional array of square girders.

The basic ideas of all the rides are the same - to provide a momentary thrill, a relief from routine, a touch of imagined glamour and excitement, daring and adventure.

CHARITY STALLS

Since the last War, a new phenomenon observed at the Fair has been the setting up of charity stalls to collect money. The only similar reference seen before the War was the British & Foreign Bible Society's stand outside the Queen's Head in 1900. Among those in recent years have been the Pinner & Harrow Round Table, Peace Committee,

Above   A powerful traction engine ready to power Harry Gray's steam yachts outside the Red Lion in Bridge Street, 1920.

Below   The Red Lion is still there in 1952, but the helter-skelter has replaced the steam yachts. The charge is 6d (2½p).

Fair Enough?

Above   The Round Table Charity stall in 1950, collecting money to send a child
to recuperate from TB in Switzerland .

Below   A slack day in Bridge Street in the 1950s.

Scouts, Church Army, United Nations Association, Canine Defence League, The Grail, Harrow & Uxbridge Lions, RNLI, Ruislip Methodist Church, World Dog Defence Fund, Watford Gospel Team, British Polio Fellowship, Pinner Sea Cadets, Cystic Fibrosis and the Pinner Association.

EPILOGUE
As the screams die away and the lights flicker out and the horses stop their stately galloping, the showmen cannot put their feet up and rest. The hours before dawn are filled with hard grafting as they dismantle each ride in orderly progression and stack it on the lorries. Each piece must be stowed correctly or it will not fit and cannot be found at the next 'tober'. As it is dismantled, too, each piece is inspected for any signs of damage or wear, to ensure the safety of riders at the next location. Hundreds of light bulbs have to be checked and if necessary replaced. Prizes are stowed away, canvases rolled up, swifts dismantled and the horses and ladybirds and teacups are unbolted.

By four in the morning, the queue of departing vans has gone and all is silent except for the fluttering of crisp papers and rattle of tin cans. Pinner Fair is over for another year.

At dawn the sweepers arrive and clean away the rubbish and hose down the streets. In 1979, 29 workmen swept the streets, earning £270 in treble overtime for three hours' work. When the first commuters walk to the station, the High Street is clean and fresh and for once free of cars; but it soon returns to normal and the sounds of *Lady of Spain* from the Gavioli organ remain only a happy memory, as the real world returns and cars jostle for parking spaces and the shop doors open once more.

CHAPTER III

THE GAFFERS

THE SHOWMEN

Faced with proposed legislation about the standards of caravans, the showmen joined together in 1899 and formed the United Kingdom Van Drivers Protection Association to fight the Bill, which was dropped. By 1910 they had changed their name to the Showmen's Guild, and this body still controls the actions of the showmen and arbitrates in cases of dispute. In some towns, it even runs the Fair.

Most of the men who come to Pinner are members of the Guild, though occasionally outsiders do find room. There was an ugly situation in 1957 when it was rumoured that "undesirable persons" had taken possession of the good sites and were yielding them up only for a consideration. There was further trouble in 1961, when the Council's new scheme to allocate spaces ran into teething troubles and some pitches were double booked. There are suggestions that as the Fair belongs to Pinner any rate-payer can set up his stall and trade during the Fair; but in practice the sites are now firmly controlled by the Council, who issue permits. Occupying a site for two years gives "squatter's rights" but generally the showmen inherit the sites and only pass them on to someone else if they decide they cannot manage to reach Pinner in time or if they prefer an even more profitable location.

Their nomadic life is by no means an easy one. However opulent their caravans, they are still travelling from place to place and not many of us would enjoy living out of a suitcase. Sites to store their caravans and equipment through the winter are becoming increasingly difficult to find, as people object to clutter in towns or intrusions into the Green Belt. They have to pay ever-increasing rents for their pitches: originally, they paid a toll to the Lord of the Manor on goods sold; then they paid a small toll to the village constable to compensate for any damage and rubbish left behind. In 1960 the Harrow Council assumed the responsibility of allocating pitches (in place of the free-for-all that had previously ensued) and charged 1/- (5p) a foot frontage for the ordinary stalls. By 1992 this had risen to £3 with more for the larger and more profitable rides. The owner of a juvenile roundabout and other attractions in 1992 paid £400 in advance for her pitches.

In response to complaints about exorbitant charges in the evenings, one showman explained the sudden surge in prices as a safety device to relieve crowd pressure and avoid possible accidents.

The showmen have also to allow for heavy insurance premiums, for public liability. These have been raised by the Council in recent years following several large awards for compensation elsewhere.

As long ago as 1868, a new roundabout could cost as much as £15,000; and the mind-boggling costs of modern technology and the improved rides now possible go some way to explaining the increased charges for rides - one recent purchase set its new owner back some £300,000.

In the old days, traction engines were expensive items. They had to take on water every eight miles and could travel at only 15 m.p.h. In the days of toll roads they had to pay as much as £10 at toll gates between Fairs.

It must not be forgotten, either, how seasonal is the work: there is little income in the winter months when work is scarce. Even in Summer, Fairs are not held every day of the week, and many Fairs are not as well patronised as at Pinner.

Whilst the date remained the Wednesday of Whit-week attendances often fell dramatically if the Fair did not coincide with half-term holidays, as in 1967, and it was this that led to the Fair being moved by order of the Home Secretary in 1972 to the Wednesday after the new Spring Bank Holiday.

A European Cup match on TV kept people away in thousands in 1979, and a wet night added to the poor turn-out. Nearly a hundred years earlier, in 1883, the Fair coincided with an equally popular one at Hillingdon, and both suffered.

In 1914, most of the showmen found that their horses or vans had been requisitioned for war work. Another blow was the introduction in 1930 of a £60 annual licence fee for owners of traction engines.

Rivalry between different showmen has often led to fights and court appearances, even in the same family. On one occasion earlier this century, a showman was arrested and taken to Pinner police station after a domestic argument, and his colleagues besieged the station in an attempt to rescue him.

Showmen are experts at solving problems. In 1954, one found a new lamp-post had been erected on his usual pitch; so he built his stall round it, with the lamp protruding from the top of his tent. Another built his stall round a zebra-crossing beacon, and used the light to help illuminate his goods.

A new light on the particular problems of the travellers was shown recently when one stallholder explained that before she could open up her small roundabout, every mount would have to be washed as she had just come from Hampstead Heath's Bank Holiday Fair, and all the horses and carriages were covered in dust.

Lest we begin to feel too sorry for the stallholders, perhaps we should mention the 1909 report in the local paper, in which a hoop-la man declared that he made only 50% profit on the operation. "If he confesses to that," said the paper, "how much more did he not confess?"

Some of the caravans were luxurious, especially that owned by Mr Fred Gray, who supervised the erection of his rides in Bridge Street whilst dressed in a smart grey suit, smoking a cigar, and sporting a waxed moustache.

Coming year after year, the showmen become well-known to local residents. In the 1930 s, a lady from Howard Place in Love Lane used to hold a tea-party for the travellers' children.

A list of some of the show men and women is given on pages 72 & 74: the Smith family are particularly well represented, but one family has always been regarded with particular affection, that of Pettigrove. The family has been coming since before 1883, running the favourite carousel by the church every year for over a century (see page 52).

In 1870 James Pettigrove bought a steam-driven Velocipede, the roundabout on which riders pedalled bicycles instead of riding astride horses. Two years later, he bought a steam-driven 3-abreast "Dobby", the type of familiar carousel we all know and love. Clearly, he was in the fore-front of innovation in those days. Thankfully, other members of the family, like George and Richard, have maintained the machinery and the beloved carousel still dominates the High Street each year. The family has done much to fight for the preservation of Pinner Fair as an institution. It was an earlier Pettigrove, Thomas, who uprooted the trees planted by Daniel Hill of Church Farm in 1897 (see page 82) and who opened up the sheep pen and released the animals that he claimed had been put in the High Street to obstruct his vehicles, though we do not really know if the sheep were intended to preserve the Fair or to stop it. One showman was blamed for cutting down some trees planted for the Coronation of Edward VII, but a local boy was later found to have been responsible. The Pettigroves were in the news again in their tractor accident in 1919.

Showmen have occasionally been up before the local Bench, one being fined 10/- (50p) for a roundabout offence in 1900, 30/- for cruelty to a horse in 1903 and 10/- for having an unlicensed locomotive the following year. These offences did not necessarily occur in Pinner, however. One unnamed roundabout owner, accused of short-changing a customer in the 1950s is said to have driven up to the court in his limousine and, being fined £2, to have asked for time to pay.

One showman likely to have remembered Pinner Fair was Jack Wakefield of Oldham. In 1954, he was taken to hospital at Northwood suffering from pneumonia.

Another was Abraham Buckland, who ran a coconut shy. Whilst the Fair was in progress on June 7th 1933, his wife Martha went into labour in their caravan and the following morning when the other caravans were moving out, they had a baby boy. The doctor confined the mother to bed for two weeks, as was the custom then, and the caravan had to remain parked on the pavement in Bridge Street all that time. The boy was baptised in the caravan by the Vicar, Rev. P. D. Ellis, and given the names Percy Pinner Buckland. For the next few years the family were invited to tea at the vicarage; but sadly Percy Pinner died at the age of five. While mother and baby were in the caravan they received a constant stream of visitors, as people brought gifts to the infant as if they were taking part in a Christmas nativity play. Mothers did the washing and brought food for the family.

Nearly a hundred years earlier, at the Coronation Fair in Hyde Park in 1838, a gingerbread seller gave birth to a son and called him "Hyde Park". They too had to stay behind when the Fair departed, and they too received many visitors.

When the Vicar, the Rev. C. E. Grenside, died in 1933, his funeral at the Parish Church on the day before the Fair was attended by a large number of the showmen.

One thing guaranteed to rile the genuine Fair showmen is to confuse them with gipsies. Perhaps in earlier days, many stalls were run by gipsies, but the showmen of today are craftsmen and proud of their traditions and their image. After the First World War, for instance, they made many friends by their action in placing a wreath on the Pinner War Memorial, accompanied by a red, white and blue banner with the words, "In loving memory of our dear Old Comrades who fell in the Great War, from the showmen of Pinner Fair." A similar inscription was left there in 1923, but in the following year they went even better. A wreath of lilies and pink carnations bore the legend, "In memory of the Fallen of Pinner, from the Pinner Showmen." By 1927 the message had been amended to "In loving memory of Pinner Heroes." The wreath had been permanently enclosed in a glass case.

In 1954 one stallholder inadvertently covered the War Memorial with the supports for his stall and aroused the wrath of villagers, but the trouble was soon rectified and was not repeated.

GIPSIES

As the showmen moved from Fair to Fair, from Hampstead to Pinner and on to Epsom for the Derby, they lived of necessity in mobile homes. Dwelling as they did in caravans, they inevitably brought out the worst fears in newspaper reporters searching for a new cliché that could be repeated for the next ten years without the tiresome necessity of having to visit the Fair itself. "Caravans" meant gipsies and their reading of George Borrow was recalled:

> "For the space of twenty-four hours, the picturesque thoroughfare, whose projecting storeys and gabled roofs are the cynosure of the eyes of antiquaries, was given over to the descendants of Lavengro."

That was in 1922; much earlier, in 1896, the condescensions of the reporter found voice in this:

> "At an early hour on Wednesday morning the High Street was alive with the voices of the early rising Bohemians, who were here with the worldly intention of lightening the pockets of the villagers, busy with the unpacking of their wares and necessary utensils, which - to say the least - were generally of a very mediocre description; frying-pans without handles were prevalent, why, we could not say, unless it be that it facilitates the packing, or gives more room. Of course, we can see why they use pieces of looking-glass instead of whole ones, and combs minus a majority of teeth in their al-fresco toilets. Their caravans are not capable of holding all whole utensils; therefore they must break the articles purposely and distribute the pieces among their relations, whose name is legion. Their system of living is very coarse, but exceptionally good, when we notice the steaks, and eggs and bacon, with other comestibles, which played sad havoc with our own olfactory nerves, and hurried us home to breakfast.

> "There are black sheep, however, generally in every flock, and our gipsies are not exempt from the metaphorical appellation; there were some so black - dirty

Fair Enough?

- that our great soap-making firms would scarcely supply sufficient of their commodity to eradicate the growth of ages; some children were running about with neither shoes nor stockings, the incrustations of dirt, we suppose, protecting their feet from injury by the flints; the parents would first require a mallet and chisel to remove sufficient of the filth to permit the soap to act. The preparations completed, the "good old annual" took place in due course, and being a fine day, strange to say, the locality of the booths for assaults-at-arms, shooting at eggs and bottles etc., with guns warranted seldom to carry straight, and cartridges equally inaccurate, the cokernut shies, the swings and roundabouts, and in short, everywhere was crowded, until the old church clock - which has to answer for the stoppage of many, and we trust yet many more, Fairs and galas at Pinner - tolled the closing hour."

The following year, pursuing his theme, he wrote:

"A great difference was remarkable in the various caravans, some appearing clean and healthy, while others were squalid to an extreme, with children almost naked and whose boots were away at their "uncle's residence[10]." The domestic arrangements were noted in detail, too, especially the absence of handles to their frying pans. "One family were, owing to circumstances, compelled to abjure the domestic plate, the deficiency being atoned for by all six of them sitting round a frying pan without a handle and each taking a piece of food from that utensil as required; it was funny if not elegant."

By 1904 the reporter was a little more appreciative:

"The morning was spent as usual by the owners of the travelling halls of amusement in covering the ground for the business of the afternoon and evening, and this work was accomplished with the dexterity born of practice, and by the early afternoon the stalls were laden with the sweetmeats which recalled the year-upon-year routine.

"The travelling tribes of Europe and Asia are not up-to-date in their sense of changing customs - they are a link with the old world and the dainties that meet the eye on the stalls bright in possession of multi-coloured sweets, gorgeous blue globes with gold and red cords, and all the artistic souvenirs of earthenware and mats and mirrors."

In 1906 a gipsy woman, Mrs. Clark, was seen to telegraph for a ¼ cwt of confetti, giving her address as "Clark, Pinner": her caravan being parked opposite the post office, that, she thought, was sufficient address. The report that year gave a gentler account, almost idyllic in its picture of men polishing brass rods on the caravans, tending to the naphtha lamps and seeing to the horses, whilst the mothers curled their children's golden tresses and fathers shaved, sitting on the steps. "Even gipsies shave sometimes," explained the rather surprised reporter.

An eye-witness who was a child in the 1930 s remembered walking past the caravans parked nose to tail in Chapel Lane, each with its chicken coop slung underneath and

10 i.e. the pawnbroker's

the hens running loose in the road.

"The occupants seemed to spend a lot of their time preparing meals and cooking on gas stoves, for most of the caravans had tanks of gas attached to the rear. For all their busy chores, they always had time to talk or call out greetings to the passers-by."

A similar kindly view of the nomads is given by Dorothy Brame in *The Villager* No. 70 in July 1961:-

"They come at night as camels to an oasis, and this oasis of noise and dust, sweat and smell, colour and cash, will be the village of Pinner on the morrow.

The families in their old, or new, comfortable caravans which have small windows crammed with frilled net and artificial flowers, spill out their water cans, calor gas drums, dustbins and most docile-looking dogs on long chains. These dogs lie patiently on mats by the startling notices of "Beware of the Dog," and guard or sleep the hours away awaiting their master's pleasure.

In the morning these visitors of ours are all among us, yet quite separate and conspicuous, especially the very young children, gay and unaccompanied by chiding mothers, pushing their glossy prams or riding small brilliant bicycles along the paths, and every now and again stopping to play on the pavement as if in their own back yards. Their slightly older brothers climb and festoon the only public tree in the village, while our own boys watch with awe and envy before being hurried on by their embarrassed mothers.

Granny stands watching and waiting, with one hand on elbow, the other embedded in nugget-brown wrinkled cheek, which long since lost the support of teeth; above her black dress, striped cardigan and floral apron she always wears a hat with great dignity.

The young mothers seem to think that their home-curled hair with a dash of peroxide here and there is still their crowning glory, and they teeter about the village on once-white, pointed, high-heeled shoes, shopping and gossiping with their highly-coloured friends.

A beautiful baby is gently rocked in a pure white pram by the large engrained hand of Grandpa, who permanently sits, not because of old age but because of the incapabilities of gross fatness; and if baby gets restless he is given Grandad's most ancient and, no doubt, most unhygienic black homburg hat to bite or chew.

The next day our visitors have gone, as quietly as they came, and, as soon as the rubbish has been collected and the dust has settled, we forget them but for one thing. For a whole year we see small blobs of yellow paint on our roads and pavements reminding us that they will be back, again and again, to the great delight of every new generation."   *(By permission of The Editor)*

Fair Enough?
PINNER FAIR IN 1935

A report in World's Fair for 22.5.1935 lists the names of the showmen taking part, and gives an idea of the range of stalls:

Gallopers (the carousel)	Mrs. T Pettigrove & Fred Gray
Helter- Skelter:	John Butlin
Swings:	F Thomas & A Stirling
Mono Rail:	Bobby Wilson
Juvenile Roundabouts:	Mr Sully
Shooting Galleries:	T Pettigrove & C Bailey
"A splendid little ride with	
twisted brass & paper organ"	A Harvey
Coconut Shies ("Sheets")	J Smith, J Lucas, Pettigrove,
	Mark Smith, M Ayres, Buckland
Palmistry & Fortune Telling:	De Cortez, Mori, Gipsy Hildon, Ram Jam Singh,
	Roseanna, Morfydd Morris, Freda & Oliver,
	Gipsy Smith, Gipsy Cooper & 7 Gipsy Lees
Midgets:	Magee
Flea Circus:	Jimmy Osborough
Freaks:	G Chadwick
?	La Nita
Limehouse Show:	Percy Cooper (with lady piper & drums)
?	Mrs. Solly Elliot (with Raymond Elliott &
	George Harris)
Lightning Artist:	Peg
Black Magic:	Captain Ludlow

Sideshows & stalls: J Glazier, J Stokes, Lowther Bros., R Wilson, S Cogger, F Herbert, W Bridges, W Manning, W Buckland, F & S Biddell, A B Buckland, W A Smith, Nolan, C Smith, A Rowe, E Woolgar, A Hobson, E L Smith, G Harvey, N Wilson, T Holmes, H Farr, J Bond, J Manning, Mrs L Crick, H Clack, T Edwards, Mrs J Mayne, A Taylor, R Green, F Harvey & J Holmes

****

Erection of stalls that year was hampered by heavy rain on the Tuesday evening and on the Wednesday morning, but the afternoon and evening were fine.

It is interesting to notice some of the names: the Pettigroves and Smiths still attend. (For Buckland, see page 68)

With 17 or more fortune tellers, it would be interesting to know if any of them foretold the coming of the War.

Compared with today, there were hardly any rides: the roundabouts, the helter-skelter, the swings and, the only concession to modernity, the "Mono Rail".

GALLOPING HORSES THE THRILL OF A

RICHARD PETTIGROVE

DO NOT EXIT
FROM THIS SIDE

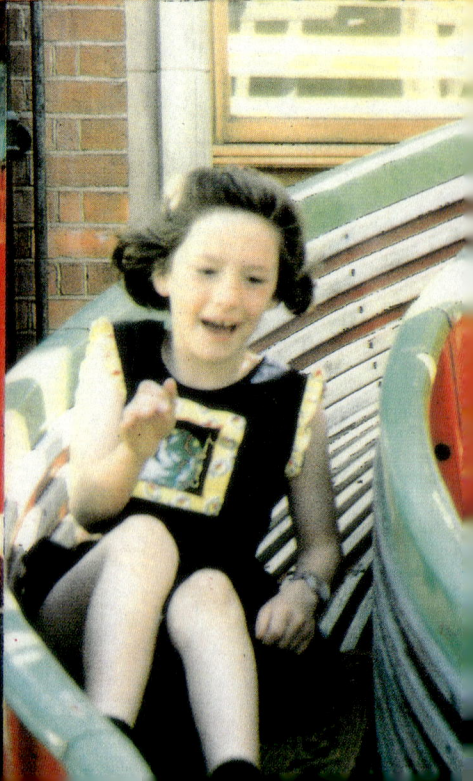

Above   Bridge Street in 1934, with a van trying to force its way through the crowds. A notice directs worshippers to the National Shrine of St Philomena at St Luke's Church.

Below   Another view of Bridge Street, in 1952. Swings and another roundabout can be seen on the corner of Chapel Lane.

Fair Enough?
THE FAIR AFTER THE WAR

In 1952, the Fair was described by *World's Fair* as "The best one-day Fair in England". though it was one of the quietest shows for years, the police estimating attendance down by 75%, and takings were low. The showmen were praised for having just come from Hampstead Fair and for dismantling so quickly. The Punch & Judy show was particularly well supported.

Among those taking part were:

Gallopers:	J Beach (with Gaudin organ) & Pettigrove
Dodgems:	Tom Smith
Autodrome:	G Beach, W Smith & Nathan Smith
Chairoplane:	Charles Abbott
Swing boats:	P Smith, Mrs Smith & Joe Smith
Noah's Ark:	Tom Benson
Juvenile roundabouts etc:	Rawlins Bros, Albert Taylor, Mr W Edwards, Charlie Edwards, J Evans, Mr Baxter, John Brixton, Alfred Harvey
Punch & Judy:	Press & Kitlee
Shows:	Appleton Bros.

(*World's Fair*, 14th June 1952)

Scenes from Pinner Fair by David Muriss

Further scenes from Pinner Fair by David Muriss.

WEATHER

On the whole the weather has been kind to Pinner Fair, though the following years were wet:

The   1880 s (in 1889 the Fair was dry for the first time for years)
        1897 drizzle all day
        1918 heavy thunderstorms in the evening
        1953 the wettest for over thirty years
        1959 heavy rain in the morning
        1960 wet in the morning, fine later
        1972 wet all day, with a cloudburst at 6 p.m. (see next page)
        1979 torrential rain in the evening
        1981 continuous rain all evening
        1982 sudden thunderstorm
        1986 cloudburst in the morning
        1989 thunderstorm

(In 1992 the thunder held over until the Friday and the day was hot and sunny).

Fair Enough?

The 1972 downpour brought forth a splendidly descriptive article in *The Villager*, written by Sarah Davies:

FAIR WEATHER

This year Pinner Fair - usually that herald of summer and bringer of blue skies - had a rather different aspect. It rained. And how it rained! It seemed somehow as though an unwritten law had been broken as the waters of the Pinn crept up their muddy banks. The promise held in the grey and threatening skies became a reality at about six o'clock in the evening when the clouds burst over the unfortunate girls screaming in the Big Wheel. Did the fairmen make a loss over this saturated event? No, for the true Pinner Fair supporter is a dogged and determined apostle of pleasure, little deterred by any prospect of wet feet and rheumatism.

The umbrellas soon appeared - striped ones and flowered ones. Then the sou'westers, sported with an air that challenged the elements to do their worst. Candy lost its floss and became a sticky pink pulp, toffee apples were rather more apple than toffee and the formerly fluffy coconuts assumed the appearance of a man who has spent a night too well on the town.

Even the bands of toughs lost some of their aura of magnificence and appeared as rather ruffled Chanticleers. The "greasers" became even more greasy with the damp which tarnished their studs and mingled the aroma of steaming leather with that of the ponies and milling bodies.

The "skinheads" perhaps regretted having joined their sect as their elastic perished and the brims of their little, perched trilby hats acted as gutters for the flowing water. But they and their garish-eyed girl friends sauntered indolently up and down Bridge Street, leaving the cowardly mums and dads in their headscarves and wellingtons crouching warily into non-existent shelter, trying desperately to enjoy their pool-like ice-creams in the blotting paper cornets and wishing that they, too, had the courage to venture out to see the "Pig-faced Woman" or even the "Two-headed Dwarf." One always does these things at Pinner Fair, after all.

Some tried to pretend that the rain wasn't there - not least of all the policemen who stood with half-shut meditative eyes in front of the haunted house - wondering, perhaps, whether their newly grown trendy side-burns were losing their curl or if the soft substance they were standing on was a not-so-hot dog or merely another religious tract.

Many were undeterred by the rain and a number of girls appeared wearing their new hot pants or cork clogs. Others even resorted to putting bags on their heads much as the far-eastern girls do with water jars. Yet the rain was everywhere, rusting the bumper cars and giving the roundabout music rather the sound of a barrel organ with wind.

One couldn't help feeling that we had a lesson to learn from the animal kingdom, several mangy canine representatives of which were lying under the caravans, fast asleep on sacks and not to be roused. Even the monkeys were huddled among their multitudinous woolly bloomers, looks of acute misery on tiny, screwed-up faces.

Certainly Pinner Fair 1972 went with a bang or at least, a fizz. The fixed smiles (or were they grimaces?) on people's faces were a clear indication of how much they were enjoying themselves. One thing did worry me. As I tried to throw the ping-pong ball into the bowl was that goldfish smiling or was it only my imagination?

(By permission of The Editor)

THE PRIZES

Early in the 19th century, the rewards for success in sporting activities at the Fair were mostly clothes: a hat, a jacket, or a smock frock. The 'slops' offered in the 1841 handbill will be instantly intelligible to any naval rating. Whips and bridles would be useful to the farmers taking part, too. (After the last war, the tradition was continued when the Round Table were offering real leather coats as prizes at their tombola stall.)

Ladies in 1839 were offered a pound of tea as an incentive to run from the Town Tree to the Red Lion and back. Food has always been a popular reward: the traditional coconuts from their first appearance in Fairs in 1879 have never ceased to be a major attraction. Earlier, men would try to climb a greasy pole for a leg of mutton (or in 1906 its value in cash if it had passed its sell-by date.) In 1947 a basket of fruit was like manna from Heaven after the privations of the war years. Sweets have always figured largely in the Fair and lollipops have often been given as consolation prizes for youngsters. In 1954, a firm in Jamaica had donated 5000 sticks of rock and these were given as compensation to unsuccessful participants in the Round Table's Lucky Dip.

Another traditional prize is the goldfish, originally given in its own glass bowl, but nowadays in its plastic bag. Today the prizes tend towards stuffed toys - some amusing gorillas were in demand in 1992 - and many a pink elephant or teddy bear has made the Fair memorable for its winner, whether given for darts, or hoop-la or in a tombola. Older residents remember taking away a budgerigar before the war. Balloons, too, given to even unsuccessful contestants, attract young customers.

Balloons frequently figure in our annals: the ones sold recently in aid of Cystic Fibrosis, the ones given away as consolation prizes, the huge inflatable in the shape of a man over McDonald's in 1992, or the boy in 1964 who strung nine balloons together, until they stretched up fifty feet into the sky. Jostled by the crowd, he lost his grip and his monster sailed upwards to some Heavenly Fairground. Does he still remember the occasion, we wonder?

During the last war, prizes were hard to come by, yet in 1942 there were chocolates and cigarettes available, along with the usual glass or china. By 1944, the war had

Fair Enough?

taken its toll, though, and visitors threw rings for such delicacies as vinegar, gravy browning, packets of dried egg or bootlaces.

In 1891, the prizes on offer included a "Town Plate". Memories of Newmarket had induced several men to run a strenuous race for it and its unveiling by the winner caused great amusement for the onlookers (see page 32). According to Edwin Ware, it was nothing more than a child's tin plate with an alphabet on it.

In recent years it has been possible to come away from the Fair clutching a TV or a CB radio. Showmen always move with the times.

The young son of a wheelwright won himself a beauty treatment as a prize from the RNLI stall in 1964.

FOOD

Among the abiding memories of Pinner Fair have always been the smells of various kinds of food: the party atmosphere extended to the idea of a mass mobile picnic, and vendors of refreshment have always been part of the scene. In the sixteenth century it may have included roast pig as in *Bartholomew Fair*, or the pagan sacrificial ox-roasting. A 1762 poem refers to 'pease porridge hot with five sausages' as staple Fair diet. Sellers of walnuts and roasted chestnuts did as good a trade at Fairs as today in Oxford Street.

Some of the early comic sporting contests in the 19th century included tests of digestion and stamina like eating as many rolls covered in treacle as possible, or sticky buns on strings. The 'Panam' stall sold brandysnaps, but along with the swings and roundabouts, one stall that became part of the tradition of the British Fair was the one selling gingerbread. Not bread at all, it was a name given in Chaucer's day to preserved ginger, and later to a kind of cake highly flavoured with ginger and made into fanciful shapes. These shapes usually were of men and women originally representing saints, and so condemned by the Puritans, and "gingerbread families" or "gingerbread husbands" figure in many accounts of Fairgrounds. To make them even more attractive, they were wrapped in "Dutch leaf". This was a kind of tinfoil, made of copper and zinc, which gave a passable imitation of gold leaf. "Gilding the gingerbread" passed into common parlance: to take the gilt off the gingerbread would be to show something for what it really was, without its tinsel trappings. Nowadays, our chocolates are wrapped in "silver" paper. The dandified gingerbread seller Tiddy-Doll became as famous at Mayfair in the 18th century.

Seaside visits are always associated with buying sticks of rock: but rock was a staple food at Fairs, too. Sweet stalls like one outside the Queen's Head were always in great demand: many of the humbugs on sale were made on the spot by the showmen, though eye-witness accounts indicate that hygiene did not always rate too highly with them:

"We used to stay and gaze at the men and women making the humbug toffee, which was dark brown and a dirty yellow. This was done by pulling a large chunk of sticky toffee into a thick snake, which was then thrown over a rusty nail and

78

they pulled it down again and kept pulling it down and throwing it over the hook. We were never allowed to have any because my mother said it was always dirty, as the men before they did it always used to spit on their hands to stop them sticking to the toffee." *(When I Was a Child* p49*).*

So much for the recollection: in fact, as Mr G P Barnes has pointed out, the hooks were not rusty: they were kept highly polished so that the rock did not stick to the metal. The hooks were of a special shape and many are still kept in the Fairground families as heirlooms. George Young remembers:

"Gosh, what delightful aromas filled the air around that stall as the toffee maker rolled, punched, pulled and twisted the yellow mixture from a large hook! Then, after rolling it into a long tail, he sliced it up into chunks with a huge cleaver,"

The modern equivalents of humbug toffees and brandy snaps are the toffee apple and the candy floss, and the latter especially has a characteristic smell that still lingers in many adult nostrils. At least one modern miss found 70p for candy floss rather too expensive, though, and preferred marshmallows.

The report in 1961 welcomed red toffee apples as well as the usual golden brown ones. The pale pink candy floss, too, had turned green for the occasion.

In the days of austerity after the last war, the Soft Drinks Industry combined to sell a kind of lemonade in bottles bearing a logo like an Underground sign. Some of the drink sold then at Pinner Fair was supplied in suspiciously soiled bottles with rusty caps, that contained liquid that would not pass the Health Inspector's standards today.

In 1885, a report noted the innovation of the sale of fried fish, and fish and chips were always staple fare, now supplemented if not replaced by sausages and onions, and ham- or beef-burgers from the burger-bar. Cockles and whelks, jellied eels and even oysters have for many epitomised the annual treat of a visit to the Fair.

CHAPTER IV

"THE PULL DOWN"

OBJECTIONS TO THE FAIR

People have objected to Pinner Fair over the years for three main reasons - inconvenience, the environment and behaviour. Some felt that it was out of keeping for a rural village to be invaded by the brash paraphernalia of a Fairground. "It was unbecoming to the dignity of the district to engage in such frivolity when it was a rising town," maintained a writer in 1906. Ten years earlier, the *Harrow Gazette* had opposed attempts to stop the Fair, maintaining that "the jolly people of Pinner" should not have to forfeit "their right to a one day's giddy frivolity out of a possible 365". In the middle of this century, a resident objected to Pinner being besieged, and another retorted that while it was an inconvenience, at least it achieved one thing: "For once the smug hideousness of Bridge Street is disguised."

The fact that the Fair takes over two main thoroughfares is of course bound to cause disruption. Although traffic is now diverted for the period of the Fair, it used to have to make its way slowly between the stalls. In 1927, "Cars and omnibuses passed through with great difficulty and passing motorists left their cars to join the merry-making." In 1932, "The police were unable to accede to the request of the Parish Council to divert the traffic, and were kept busy guiding cars through the throng. Great difficulty was experienced by Green Line coaches, and several cars were scratched. Nearly all received showers of confetti, to the annoyance of their owners." If these were open-topped tourers, one can sympathise.

Photographs in the national press in the 1930s show buses, coaches and many cars and vans trying to thread their way through the stalls in Bridge Street. From at least 1933, though, as the Fair spread further up Bridge Street, the 183 bus stopped at Cecil Park and another service ran from Waxwell Lane to Northwood. Buses would come from Northwood, turn into Waxwell Lane by the Police Station and reverse into Bridge Street to begin their return journey, but the gradual expansion of the Fair led to coconut shies being pitched near the junction, and in 1938 the Metropolitan Traffic Commissioner had to request that stalls be kept further down Bridge Street to allow room for the buses to turn.

The Green Line coaches on Route 703 were diverted along George V Avenue in 1960, as were the 98b and 209 buses. Of recent years, all traffic has been prevented from entering the area of the Fair. Previously, there had been complaints that the diversion signs had not been put up early enough. Certainly nowadays all is done to make the setting up of the stalls a speedy operation. The station car park has been closed on the Tuesday afternoon, and cars still parked in Bridge Street or the High Street have been towed away to Battersea.

The caravans of the showmen parked in nearby roads and the cars of people coming to the Fair together caused an alarming road hazard, and residents were concerned about who would be responsible if there was an accident, as seemed likely: who was in charge? This was indeed a good question, as can be seen elsewhere.

Some of the shopkeepers, especially those who have not grown up in the village, object to their loss of custom over the day of the Fair, and are concerned that the access to their shops is blocked, their light cut off or their windows damaged. Other are more philosophic, realising that the showmen are customers themselves. In earlier days, they would have needed supplies from the corn chandlers, like Woodman's. Today they need beer or cigarettes, clothes or cosmetics, food or medicine. The proprietor of one shoe shop, asked why he did not board up his stop windows against the Fair as others did, replied that a good number of the showmen came in for shoes on their visit to Pinner. The Fair customers, too, drawn in their thousands to the village, can produce a sudden increase in demand.

When the Fair did not start until mid-day, little was lost as Wednesday was an early-closing day, anyway. In any case, it is only for one day a year. The pubs usually did a roaring trade, as in 1921 and 1947 when wartime shortages were forgotten. On the Tuesday night, the workers erecting the big rides nowadays try to finish before closing time - it gives an added incentive to their work. On the night of the Fair, however, most pubs close by 7 p.m.

Inconvenience was experienced, too, by some householders who found their garage drives blocked by parked cars or vans. In former days, it might have been straying horses, as the hundreds of horses that had pulled the Fair to Pinner were turned out to graze on the verges in West End Lane and other nearby roads.

DAMAGE

One of the earliest complaints on record came in 1878 when horses bringing caravans to the Fair were tethered or left to graze in Waxwell Lane. Some of these horses had been so clever, said a correspondent to the *Bucks Advertiser*, as to lift the latch on a garden gate and trample all over the immaculate lawns, reducing them to mud. Not content with this, they had wandered into the vegetable garden and eaten the growing crops, including a bed of strawberries, and helped themselves to green apples in the orchard. From the description, this would seem to have been Waxwell Farmhouse, where Annie Trotter was later to create such a beautiful garden.

A perpetual worry for the authorities has been the possibility of damage to the roads. In the past, showmen were not above removing paving stones and digging holes to secure foundations for their stalls. Objections had been raised against Harrow Fair in the 1870 s because of showmen using crowbars to lever up pavements and dig holes in the road. In 1887, the Highways Board of the local Council issued a notice requesting "the utmost care by the proprietors of steam roundabouts and boat-swings not to damage the roads or obstruct the traffic in Pinner."

In 1890, Mr Henry, the Surveyor of the Highways for Pinner, "was energetic in the forenoon and had five or six summonses served on offenders, receiving in several other cases compensation for damage done." Tolls were exacted from the showmen as shown elsewhere, to compensate for this damage. As pavements were being damaged

Fair Enough?

each year, in 1981 the Council relaid new stronger paving blocks in Bridge Street and High Street, though it was particularly distressing to see new paving bricks damaged by heavy lorries in 1984. There was an alarm in 1985 when a crack appeared at the top of the High Street as the Fair was about to be set up, but workmen were able to ascertain that there was no likelihood of further subsidence and all went ahead as planned. At the back of local traders' minds was the anxiety about who would pay for damage, and even when the culprit was known it was sometimes difficult to extract repayment from him. Damage was done to private forecourts in 1939, but when the police were informed, they replied that some shop or pub owners (as at the Red Lion) had entered into a private agreement with the showmen and let out their forecourts privately, so it was not the concern of the police.

In 1868 Daniel Hill, the bachelor farmer at Church Farm at the top of the High Street, had offered a field for the Fair in an apparent effort to divert it away from his front door (see poem on page 8). Nearly thirty years later, he planted four trees alongside the dead Town Tree "to beautify the village". There were some who thought it possible that these had been planted to obstruct the Fair and make life difficult for the rides to be erected. The Pettigrove family have been coming to the Fair for over a hundred years and Mr J Pettigrove in 1897 was not the sort of man to let a little thing like this stand in his way. The trees and their protective fences were quickly demolished and the Fair proceeded. The local reporter plaintively muttered that it was a pity the trees had not been merely dug up, so that they could have been replanted. The Town Tree fell down of its own accord the following year.

Even today, there is a similar conflict of interest between those who want to plant trees to enhance the appearance of Pinner throughout the year and the stallholders who find branches impeding their flights of fancy, on the one day of the Fair.

It was the Pettigrove family, too, who were concerned in the Fair's most spectacular accident in 1919. Their much-loved carousel has long had a pitch just below the Church and in that year the three vans containing the equipment were being pulled by a traction engine, when the pin of the clutch came loose. The driver, Thomas Pettigrove, leapt clear as the engine started to roll out of control down the High Street. His teenaged son, however, was still on board. As he careered down the hill at fifteen miles an hour, he desperately tried to steer his engine between the half-erected stalls, and two quick-thinking showmen, James Watson and Samuel Mayne, dragged their caravans across his path. The runaway engine was brought to a halt, but a horse pulling Mr Mayne's caravan was badly injured and had to be despatched on the spot by John Lee, the butcher at No 7. The windows of two shops opposite, owned by Mr Alvey, the stationer and by Mrs Emery, the photographer, were damaged by frightened horses, but miraculously no-one was injured. Mr Alvey died two months later, but whether the shock hastened his death is not known. The affair caused great excitement, and to this day older inhabitants recall it with pardonable embroidery. The brave Pettigrove lad was rewarded by over £5 collected on the spot.

SIZE

Concern is now being expressed that the Fair is increasing as it has done for a hundred years, not only in the area of ground it covers but in the size of some of the rides. In 1961 the Council imposed limits on the extent of the Fair, though the original intention to stop it at the Marsh Road railway bridge has since been relaxed.

DANGER

It is on environmental grounds that most of the complaints have been made over the years. Health and Safety are not new concepts, and there has for some time been anxiety about the risk of an accident, like the one in 1919 above. In 1934 when a car burst into flames at the top of the High Street, the fire engine had to struggle to push its way through the crowds. The authorities now ensure that the stalls leave enough room between them for the emergency vehicles to pass, and a fire engine makes a test journey through them on the morning of the Fair. With crowds estimated at 200,000 visiting the Fair during the day, there is genuine concern about what would happen in an emergency. As rides tower over the shops and nudge against each other, little room is left between them for emergency exits to allow people to make way for a fire engine or ambulance. The local Health and Safety Executive, following the newly published Code of Practice drawn up in collaboration with the Showmen's Guild, are to carry out a Risk Assessment Survey to ensure that all is well. Much depends on their findings, which could radically alter the face of the Fair as we know it.

The more nervous among the spectators question the safety of the rides themselves, but they need not worry unduly, as long as the passengers obey the rules. A chartered engineer with special experience of Fairground equipment examines the rides in use, along with five of the Council's enforcement officers. One ride in 1992 bore the ominous words, "NO WRECKLESS RIDING"!

Although the rides seem frightening - that is their appeal, after all - they are inspected every time they are erected and dismantled. The showmen claim that in this way they are in fact safer than the rides on permanent sites, which are inspected only at the statutory 14-month intervals. The more modern the machines, too, the higher will be safety standards imposed in manufacture.

Like so many tourist attractions, though, Pinner Fair has become the victim of its own success. Some compromise will have to be reached to ensure that large numbers of people can enjoy themselves without endangering their lives.

Older residents remember the police linking hands in the High Street to form a barrier dividing up and down pedestrian flows. In 1950 there was an alarming situation when the crowd at the foot of the High Street became so great that people jumped over the fences protecting the village gardens and even waded across the River Pinn to escape being crushed. The St. John Ambulance Brigade, in their post in the old village hall, dealt with thirty casualties, and three women had to be taken to hospital. The Brigade has been attending the Fair since 1898, and has two ambulances standing by in readiness. In 1952, the widening of the bridge over the River Pinn helped considerably to relieve the pressure. The police in 1962 introduced "walkie-talkie" radios to help with crowd control.

INJURY

"I have never known anyone killed or injured at the Fair," wrote a supporter in 1985. In fact, there have been several injuries, though many fewer than the situation might suggest or alarmists fear. Friction burns and blisters are common, as, not surprisingly, are cases of fainting, dizziness or sickness.

Others have been cut or bruised when falling off rides, but none too seriously. In 1903, a London visitor, Mrs Smith, was treated for a scalp wound after falling off a roundabout. Broken ankles were suffered by two ladies in 1924, one of them being a Miss Smith, when they also fell off roundabouts. And yet another of the same name, Mrs Smith, one of the caterers, was boiling sugar to make rock in 1938 when she upset the cauldron and scalded her foot. A North Harrow lady was struck by an errant pellet from the rifle range that same year, and in 1950 another was hit by a bottle dropped from the top of the helter-skelter, but the showmen could scarcely be blamed for that incident. In 1967 a special constable on point duty in Marsh Road was knocked down and bruised by a car.

Children have been kicked by ponies (1936 & 1960) or donkeys (1952) and have been bitten by rats (1973) or monkeys (1974). In 1947, a girl tripped and fell into a plate-glass window and another cut her hand on her goldfish bowl when she fell in 1965. In 1974 a hoarding fell off a fortune-teller's stall (presumably not to her surprise) and damaged a man's leg and fingers.

Recent fatal accidents at permanent fairgrounds and football stadiums have concentrated the mind, and the thought of huge sums paid in compensation for injuries has meant that the Council now insist on high insurance premiums being paid by the showmen, with cover of up to £5m for rides and £2m for stalls. The Showmen's Guild assist their members with these payments.

HEALTH

As Fairs are manned by travelling showmen, there has long been a fear that they might bring notifiable diseases with them: a Fair at Bognor in 1871 was deserted because of a rumour that one of the showmen had smallpox. Three years later a child died of "fever" at a Horsham Fair and started a similar panic. In 1920, an anonymous correspondent to our local paper claimed, without evidence, that the Fair was a "hotbed of disease and immorality", just as Lady Northwick had asserted in 1893 (see page 108). The supporters of the Fair retorted that the Medical Officer inspected the caravans before they were allowed to enter and it was only rarely that one was turned back. In 1903, the Parish Council even took the precaution of washing the roads with disinfectant after the show.

An alarming cattle disease in 1866/67 which caused several Cattle Fairs to be abolished strengthened the beliefs of some people that some that animal infections could be spread, as horses and dogs from the Fair were allowed to roam freely.

NOISE

"Environmental pollution" is the current jargon but for years people have complained about the noise and smells engendered in the cause of merry-making. Car radios heard playing through open windows nowadays drown summer birdsong; and all-night parties and discos still disturb the sleep of thousands. We are all aware of the effects of too loud a noise, especially if it is repetitive. The furore caused when the first steam-driven organs were invented in 1865 has already been mentioned, along with the reaction to them when they invaded Pinner in the 1880s (see page 56).

Since then, for over a hundred years, the organs and amplifiers have ground out their discordant notes on one day a year, from music-hall tunes to rock music. The reaction from neighbouring houses is bound to be unfriendly, whether because the music is thought to be too loud, or because music heard at a distance is irritatingly distracting from the work in hand, or because two or more tunes are being played at once and clashing with each other, or because one tune is played with mind-bending, weary repetitiveness.

"The music continued for hours on end and aggravated sickness, driving sane persons into lunacy," wrote a sufferer in 1885.

The noise the following year "created by the proprietors of the amusements coupled with the loud music of the steam roundabouts playing the changes every few minutes of the day must have proved almost too much for the tradesmen. However, coming but once a year, this can probably be borne without a grievance." That dubious report in an 1881 Watford paper, the one that referred to the Saturday Fair, claimed that "residents in the neighbourhood would no doubt have been more enraptured with the merry-go-round and its accessories had the tuneful organ been possessed of more variety in its musical repertoire". The paper adds, though, that no-one can complain of having suffered any real annoyance while the youngsters and others "found a lot of pleasure in taking healthful equestrian exercise at the modest charge of a penny a time." The amusements are said to have been positioned in a field near the High Street, which might have accounted for extra noise.

Our own local paper in 1897 protested, "The blare of the automatic organ was somewhat objectionable to those who possess oversensitive nerves." Perhaps the reporter a few years later was being ironic when he claimed annoyance caused by the "roundabouts playing some extract from an oratorio repeated with a monotony that was almost unbearable." Four years later, in 1908, he wrote, "In the evening the fun became fast and furious, and the shrieks of the young girls, the hoarse laughter of men, combined with the music of the organ, contrived to make a pandemonium which at close quarters was remindful of Bedlam."

He went on to describe the "usual monster roundabout at the entrance to Love Lane, the organ pealing out a small variety of tunes, which must rest as musical memories to the near residents for some days to come."

Fair Enough?

Just before the first war, the roundabouts were said to have "screeched out popular ditties". Still in search of a wider vocabulary, the post-war reporter said that "the braying of roundabouts vied with the voices of the showmen, for volume, if not for quality of sound." They must have been hearty showmen to have matched the volume of the Gavioli organs in full blast.

The 1921 reporter who referred disparagingly to music from "hurdy-gurdies and orchestrions" would have offended connoisseurs of the magnificent old Fair organs.

Walter Druett, writing in 1937, maintained, "Today the annual event is little more than a raucous noise and an unmitigated nuisance to many people, but it retains its attractions and fascination for the general public." (*Pinner Through the Ages* p36).

By 1956, the Observer reporter noted the "frenzied bellowing of loudspeakers" as technology began to take over, though he still referred to "the panting shriek of steam organs." Some of the reports seem to have been written at the desk, without the writer's having been caught up in the excitement and jollity of the Fair and the peculiarly nostalgic and unique sound that issues from these machines. "Music is anathema to the people of Pinner," wrote one observer in 1980. In 1985, a patrolling policemen was heard to mutter, "It's only 10.30 in the morning and I'm on my fifth Paracetemol of the day."

From the 1926 Panatrope, sound amplification has developed into the multi-decibel monsters of today, each competing to burst the ear-drums of youths attuned to Walkmen and ghetto-blasters. Beside them the old mechanical organ seems positively quaint and subdued, and one wonders what all the fuss was about. Fuss there certainly was, and the noise was such as to cause protests to the Home Secretary with the result described on page 108 Again in 1897 his successor replied to complaints by saying, "It was not considered necessary or advisable to abolish the roundabouts, but where the steam music proved a nuisance, an application for its abatement would have a hearing."

We are not, of course, alone in having a noisy Fair. In 1926, a fearful home owner in Sudbury anticipated the coming Easter Fair in Eton Avenue: "We shall again be menaced at all hours of the day by what in some quarters may be termed 'music'. This is in every conceivable way a nuisance." One perhaps hears the same comment today from villagers invaded by an ecstatic all-night rave party in a muddy Wiltshire field.

A Fair at Welling, Kent, was objected to in the 1930's because of "the nerve-racking noise which disturbed the sleep of children until a late hour, caused by the running of traction engines, the screeching of sirens, the clanging of bells and other ungodly dins." Walk alongside any main road locally today and you will hear much the same.

The noise of the donkey engines and, later, the whirr of diesel generators are frequently mentioned in reports. Above all sound the (inevitably) "raucous" shouts of the hucksters crying for custom: "The ear-splitting cries of the coconut men" startled the ears in 1885 as they do today.

Visitors to the Fair add their own contribution in screams of ecstasy or the cries of lost children. In earlier days, they bought penny hooters, trumpets, cornets or squeakers, and long before party-poppers were invented went around deafening the ears of all their neighbours. Children bought drums to torment their parents still further.

It was not only during the Fair that noise caused trouble. In the 1950 s residents complained about the showmen arriving early and shouting, clattering poles and revving engines. Their "lurcher dogs" barked and set off the domestic hounds to follow suit. There was a growing feeling at that time, though, that the showmen were taking advantage of the relaxations of restrictions that had been allowed throughout the war years.

The ever-popular rifle ranges, too, added to the "wild tumult". "Shots from the rifle ranges startled the imaginative," said a writer in 1912.

SMELLS

The noisy machines also emitted unpleasant smells: diesel and carbon dioxide fumes today replace the pungent odours of paraffin, acetylene or the even earlier naphtha oil lamps of the last century. (The latter, invented by a Huddersfield man, came to London in the 1850 s and incidentally provided a fire hazard of potentially alarming proportions.)

The over-used urinal by the old Red Lion in Bridge Street gave rise to complaints in 1956, and the general shortage of public toilets is a constant nightmare. During the last war, the village hall then at the foot of the High Street had a toilet, but it was used by A.R.P. Wardens, who objected to the public being given access to it.

Many memories of a happier kind about Pinner Fair are centred on the smell of food: candyfloss has its own particular aroma, and when this is overlaid with fish and chips, hamburgers, hot dogs and onions, all spiced with oil fumes, the effect is unforgettable. The first appearance of fried fish in 1885 was disliked for this reason:

"Scent fountains or 'ladies' tormentors', as they are termed in some quarters, were plentifully used by the young of both sexes. It could have been wished that the fountains contained real scent, as they might have been drowned by the smell of fried fish which issued from one of the stalls. The odour of fried fish is not particularly agreeable at the best of times, but on a warm summer's evening, when the appetite is not very keen, it is decidedly objectionable. This seems to be a new feature, and the sooner it is abolished the better, otherwise the affection of the public for Fairs may be estranged altogether from them."

(Harrow Gazette 30th May 1885)

CROWD BEHAVIOUR

There were some years, however when all was not so peaceful. The large crowds attracted to the Fair inevitably bring with them problems of their own, not only in the congestion and over-crowding of narrow streets, but by their behaviour.

Fair Enough?

The Fair used to start only after the shops closed at mid-day. In 1906, for instance, all was not ready until 3 p.m. Then came "the families of the elite who wish to avoid the rough and tumble business in the evening when the lights are low," sons no doubt in sailor suits and daughters clasped firmly by the hand lest they be spirited away to white slavery. In the last century, the gentry would patronise the Fair in the early evening with their dinner guests in evening dress but generally it has been the rule that the afternoon (or, latterly, the mornings) were for the younger children, others coming later:

> "In the afternoon as usual, the children held sway and right merrily did the youngsters enjoy the sport and their eyes gleam at this to them entrance of real pantomime in their midst....On the departure of the children, the young men and women troop in from Harrow, Eastcote, Ruislip, Northwood and Wealdstone and make life merry with their laughter and pleasantries, these consisting almost wholly of "brushing" the faces of the passers-by, who received the kind attention in accordance with the temper of the moment."

The "brushing" referred to above was a form of torment, with a tickling stick, of the kind like a feather duster made famous by Ken Dodd. Sometimes made from a cardboard tube out of which popped feathers or paper when activated, or from a piece of copper wire a yard long and costing a penny, they were used by both sexes to tickle the faces of others in the crowd In 1906, a reporter, whilst buying a "fairing", was slapped on the cheek with a "tiddler" and tickled behind the ear with a feather.

The party atmosphere of the Fair in Victorian and Edwardian days led to "a solid jam wearing absurd hats, blowing on absurd whistles and shrieking hooters and throwing away money on absurd competitions." The main attraction for the young men seems to have been the tormenting of the opposite sex by what were called "ladies' tormentors", "scent fountains[11]", "squirts" or "leaden tubes". Basically they were a form of elementary water pistol. The writer in 1885, as will be recalled, commented that it was a pity they were not filled with real scent to drown the odour of fried fish. Eleven years later, the *Gazette* thundered:

> "Those abominations, the leaden tubes, filled with we know not what, were in full go and not only spoilt the tempers of the old folks who received some of the contents, but also spoilt the shirt-fronts and fineries and fal-de-rals of the males and females assembled. It were better that squirts were relegated to some distance from the village on Fair day; the juniors who like that class of fun could then drown themselves and each other in aqua - not pura - to their hearts' content."

In 1901, there were complaints about the use of dirty water in 'squirts' on friend or stranger alike, and the "height of enjoyment for many" was a pig's bladder on the end of a stick, a device handed down through the centuries from the king's jester - the equivalent today of being struck over the head with a balloon.

---

11 The scent fountains could be bought by the showmen from firms like Brinkleys or Phillips of Aldgate or from Bath & Co of Homerton at 2/9 (145p) a gross and sold for a penny each, a profit of over 300% .

As in other areas, there were probably also chestnut fights: one at Guildford in 1863 had turned into a riot.

CONFETTI

Around the turn of the century, however, a new menace crept in for the young ladies visiting the Fair, the throwing of confetti; and its use persisted up to the last war. Young men and women both used it, to scatter over and then to stuff down the clothing of anyone in the crowd. Confetti battles, like miniature snowfights, raged fast and furious. This was of course in the evenings.

Girls coming home from the Fair would be made to stand on a piece of newspaper on the kitchen floor to collect all the offending scraps while they undressed: boys had to do this in the back yard.

Apparently, some young people were carried away by the excitement and forgot to include the confetti when they stuffed their hands rudely where they should not have been.

Reports vary widely about how these torments were received. "The girls certainly enjoyed it," claims one octogenarian. In 1919 ladies engaged in mock confetti battles with wounded Anzac soldiers from Pinner Place nursing home. In 1920 the fun was "fast and furious: the quaint old High Street was a whirl of gaiety". In 1932, "animated scenes were witnessed at the Fair: in the evening confetti battles were furiously waged, but in spite of the pushing and crowding everyone was good humoured and laughter permeated the hour." But it was in that same year that a worried councillor spoke of "scenes of brutality and indecency such as never seen before." Girls had apparently been picked up and shaken to make sure the confetti was well and truly involved in their clothing. Two years later, an indignant lady complained of violence and assault on young girls whom she had seen struggling on the floor with their clothes torn:

"SIR, As a newcomer to the district I was attracted to Pinner this evening by what I had heard described as "Pinner's Old Village Fair" but if the happenings I saw there were according to the customs of the old days I am afraid that since a child I have been disillusioned. As a woman with a full sense of the proprieties of life I was, frankly, disgusted at what I saw. A large number of youths were there and their one ambition, apparently, was to push at any young woman who came their way, close with her, with only one intention in view. Some of them, it is true, had a small amount of confetti in their hands but this was used, it seemed, to help lay the dust on the ground. This obscene and disorderly behaviour was carried on in the eyes of the police, who I suppose, deem the "Fair" to be a legitimate cloak for any unseemly behaviour.

"If a man assaulted a woman in broad daylight in the middle of Pinner High Street on any other day he would be inside the police station in the twinkling of an eye and the arm of the law would be patting itself on the back.

Fair Enough?

"There was one poor girl in particular who attracted my attention and gained my pity. Two louts had dragged her to the ground and had torn her clothes in their actions. When I reached her she was crying, and her "admirers" looked upon me as a prude who had no right to interfere. When I remonstrated with them they ran off quickly, and turned their attentions to another victim.

"Some might say the girls are to blame, but if they are all like that I am glad I am one of the prudent ancients and not one of the so-called modern young women, who, if the assertion is correct - I know it is not - are a disgrace to their sex. I was so upset that I resolved to express my feelings at once so that, if you deemed to publish my letter, some of these young men I saw might feel ashamed - if that is possible."

(Pinner, Wednesday May 18, 1934)

A case, apparently, of the arm of the law turning a blind eye whilst scratching its chin.

The Parish Council in 1932 had protested violently about the hooliganism, and the following year there was very little. The Pinner Association complained to the Harrow Urban District Council soon after the formation of both bodies that though they were in favour of the continuance of the Fair, they deplored the use of confetti and water pistols and thought the Fair would be far more pleasant if these were abandoned. The Showmen's Guild suggested notices banning the use of both tortures. All other large Fairs, they said, had banned their use: they no doubt realised that being tormented was not always an attraction for possible customers. As usual, the problem was passed on to the police, who said they had no authority to ban the sale of any particular article and that they could only prosecute offenders if an official complaint had been lodged with them.

The Council consulted the Ministry of Health about the current wave of "impropriety and rowdyism" in 1935, mentioning in particular the assaults in varying degrees on young females by means of confetti and water pistols, and asked for suggestions on how to deal with the menace. The Ministry replied that as the Fair was held at Pinner in a public place, there were bye-laws in operation governing behaviour in public. These would include provisions dealing with "profane, indecent, violent or abusive language or conduct or shouting by hawkers, the use of stink bombs or the squirting or scattering of offensive liquids or powder and the depositing of litter to the detriment of public amenities." The provisions of the Metropolitan Police Act would also apply.

Suggestions by the Council that the Fair Charter could be amended to ban confetti were discounted on the grounds that the Charter did not concern itself with conduct at the Fair, merely its dates of operation. The absence of particular wording in the Charter was deplored in other connections as well.

Confetti torments stopped with the war and the Fairs after the war were quieter for some years, apart from the panic in 1950 referred to above. At Shrove Tuesday celebrations in Munich, confetti battles still occur today.

IMMORALITY

Immorality has been mentioned in passing. Other more qualified analysts can dilate on the sublimation of passion through tickling sticks or thrusting handfuls of paper down a blouse. The proximity of thousands of bystanders is probably as good a safeguard as any against too much impropriety. As George Ellement wrote in 1920, when it was suggested that the Fair be moved to a field: "Is it not far better to have your Fair in a well-lighted public place than in a field which is unlighted ...and insufficiently police-patrolled?"

Certainly the lights of an early summer's evening are part of the attraction: Howard Spring wrote in *The Villager* in 1943 that "The chief glory of the Fair was the concentrated fierceness of electric light (which) burned down on everything." He presumed the Fair would not have survived the war because of the black-out, but it did, closing only with darkness. Some parishioners before the war noted that the roads were better lit on Fair days than during the rest of the year. One cottage in Bridge Street used to enjoy the unaccustomed luxury of electric light from the generators outside their front door by way of compensation for the blocking of their view.

Behind some of the bright lights, however, some questionable entertainments have been seen from time to time, and abolitionists have seized, with alacrity, on these as weapons. Evidence is hard to come by, as few customers have voiced their opinions. In 1959 there was a rumour that strip tease had turned into nude displays: but the ephemeral nature of Fair folk is such that little can be done about it until next year. "I have never seen anything immoral at the Fair," wrote one defender in 1920. Perhaps he had stayed with the coconut shies.

The Relief of Mafeking in May 1900 perhaps helped that year's Fair to pass without incident, but the following year was another matter. Did people feel the urge to celebrate a new century or feel that Grandmother Victoria's eye was no longer on them? For whatever reason, the Fair was unusually disorderly. The reinforced police had their work cut out dealing with a free fight, and four men were arrested for being drunk and disorderly. The village did not quieten down until well after the usual closing time of 11 p.m. All this was in spite of the

> "public dancing exhibitions to the melody of concertinas, and the continual grinding out of the National Anthem from the roundabouts. Many were drunk, insulting the more respectable members of the crowd: next morning they paid the penalties for insobriety. The Fair was not a success and is clearly on the decline."

We are reminded of a mediaeval Bishop of Salisbury, who protested about "dances or vile and indecorous games which tempt to unseemliness."

The wording of the 1859 petition against Harrow Fair (see page 99) is also worth studying in this connection.

Fair Enough?

DRINK

Although reference has been made to the pubs formerly being open all day and doing a roaring business, drunkenness has not featured largely in police or newspaper reports. When the Cocoa Tree Temperance Tavern opened just in time for the Fair in 1878, it did a roaring trade, its "good quality articles" for sale attracting more customers than the pubs. At the presentation of the petition of 1893 (see page 108), the defence stated that there had been no charges for being drunk over the past ten years. One of the Pinner J.P.'s explained that this was because there was no Pinner[12] lock-up and anyone charged had to be taken six miles to the nearest one. Drink was, of course, a major social problem in the last century, and the Salvation Army were to the forefront of campaigns to stop Fairs for this reason. Hence, perhaps, the popularity of the "Aunt Sally" shies, based on figures from the Army. Certainly there was said to be less trouble at the Fair in 1917-18 when beer was in short supply.

LITTER

A constant source of irritation has been the amount of litter left behind, but a well organised local authority now sees to this before most residents are awake on the Thursday morning. Unusually, in 1966 the Cleansing Department left behind a great deal of rubbish in the streets; but today the roads and pavements are hosed down by six in the morning. At least these days the street cleaners do not have to cope with the matted refuse of wet confetti and horse manure of former years.

PARASITES

Nineteenth century complaints about the stall holders were relatively scarce, apart from a few mutterings about gipsies. Generally it was felt that the showmen were no trouble, though on one occasion when one was arrested, his fellows besieged the police station in an effort to release him. Perhaps not all would go so far as Mr Ernest Edwards of Haydon Hall who in 1920 claimed a long association with the showmen: "My experience of them is that a more honest good-hearted, moral set of people one could not wish to find." What complaints did arise were often about the hangers on: "The worst feature of the day is the large number of the lounger type which are attracted, which (sic) make it their sole business to hang like parasites on the heels of the real workers wherever they go." That was in 1897; twenty five years earlier, it was thought that "the shows and exhibitions of which these Fairs consist and the persons who own them, and those who always follow in their wake, have a tendency to demoralise and degrade the class of persons for whom they are intended, particularly the young people of that class."

In 1879, the Fair was attended by "several respectable people from Pinner and a large number of roughs". Lady Northwick in 1893 complained about the Fair being attended by 'people from Whitechapel'.

In 1956, to show that attitudes to Pinner Fair seldom change over the years, a resident wrote to the Council objecting, not to the showmen, but to "the fortune hunters in their

12 Pinner Police Station was not opened until 1899

92

wake". The police replied, when consulted, that it would be unfair to ban the itinerant sellers of balloons and paper hats.

CRIME

Mr Edwards's letter quoted above was in answer to the same anonymous correspondent, already mentioned, who had not only feared disease and immorality, but claimed that the Fair "attracted every thief and ruffian for twenty miles". A 1926 complaint at Sudbury referred to the peace being "disturbed by hooligans who congregage at holiday times."

"Gipsies, Bohemians and Nomads" was a typical description by the rather supercilious reporters of the last century, who specialised in pointing out the contrasts in the life-style of the traveller (see page 69).

Police records, as a matter of interest, deny that the Fair has attracted more than its share of thieves, though there is usually a smattering of purses or wallets lost or thefts of or from cycles. In 1906, a detective was imported especially to guard against pick-pockets and had his own watch and chain lifted. Fashions change, and over the years we see an occasional stallholder being arrested for gambling, such as John French who in 1914 was fined 10/- (50p) for gambling with dice and a coloured cloth.

Richard Tarling had been sentenced to fourteen days' hard labour in 1864 (see page 47) so perhaps John French was lucky to live in more enlightened times. As recently as 1945, a woman from Greenford was fined £1 for conducting a Roll A Penny stall at the Fair and a Hounslow man 10/- (50p) for a similar offence - he had claimed he was only minding the stall for his absent brother.

A variation of the usual pattern was noted in a police-court case in 1919 when a 12-year-old boy stole £10 from a shoemaker's shop in St Ann's Road, Harrow and was later apprehended at Pinner Fair, still with eight of the stolen pounds intact. He had spent the other £2 on ice creams and having a good time. For that money one imagines he could in those days have sampled most of the rides in the Fair several times over.

Reports from elsewhere of illegal horse-trading and con-men, of ringing the changes, passing false coinage and other sharp practices, were no doubt reflections of what happened here as well.

A respectable hay-dealer of Pinner, William Abrey, was arrested at a Fair in Kingston, Surrey, in 1856. He had handed over some gold coins for meat, but the dealer tested the coins on a machine and found them to be counterfeit. A policeman accused him of being a "regular smasher" (a passer of false coinage) but his innocence was proved when the Bank accepted that the coins were genuine.

In 1984, one lad was fined £175 for obstruction when he refused to leave a ride. Perhaps he had calculated how much he was paying for each second of dizziness.

Fair Enough?
VIOLENCE

Within the last thirty years, fashion has decreed other causes for concern as gang warfare became the rage. In 1964, the police were warned of likely head-on clashes between rival groups of leather-clad motor cyclists, the "Rockers" and their opposite numbers, the tee-shirted "Mods" on scooters. The large police presence helped to thin out any accumulations of youths and the threatened conflicts were avoided. One ride was closed down when Rockers surrounded it whilst it was occupied entirely by Mods. Thirty youths were arrested, charged with carrying offensive weapons, or using threatening behaviour or insulting language. The weapons included studded belts and knives, though the youths claimed the latter were for "scraping the carbon off the cylinder heads" of their motorcycles and one boy protested that his trousers were about to fall down when his vicious-looking belt was confiscated.

Later manifestations, in the shape of "Greasers" and "Skinheads" again threatened trouble in 1972, but here the weather played a decisive part (see page 76).

We have found no sign here of the kind of riots so graphically described by George Sanger elsewhere in the middle of the last century, as at Newport, Mon., in 1839, when 30,000 Chartists advanced on the Fair intent on damage, but were driven off by two dozen soldiers. Nor have we suffered the extraordinary violence seen at Hampstead in 1819 when a gang of 200 roughs bludgeoned all who visited the Fair and removed their surplus jewellery, money and even clothing. Gangs of youths attacked the Fair at Bath in the 1830s and at Stalybridge twenty years later miners kicked a gingerbread seller to death with their clogs.

Heavy police presence has generally ensured a relatively peaceful day and typical comments from the press are: "A quiet day with no arrests"; "no noticeable disturbance during the day"; "no serious charge was ever brought against any person on Fair day since time immemorial" (this in 1896); "a large contingent of police was on duty, although the trouble free way in which the occasion is carried on rarely calls for any intervention." 130 police were on duty in 1992.

With all these "many attendant evils", those who object to the Fair have plenty of ammunition. From the brutal treatment of donkeys in 1872 to the worries over safety in 1992, headaches abound. "Twenty years ago there used to be just low-lying stalls," explained a worried official recently. "All this heavy machinery is getting away from the original intention of the Fair." But then, we probably always have been, if we ever knew what that was.

Fairs generally have been on the decline for over two hundred years: once shops were opened for a regular supply of goods, there was less need for annual Trading Fairs. The 1871 Act speaks of Fairs that are "unnecessary" as being eligible for abolition. Many Trade Fairs, though, turned to amusements as happened in Pinner, and catered for labourers and apprentices, in spite of attempts by employers to stop them. Harrow's Fair was stopped in 1872 and many other great Fairs have faced strong opposition. The greatest of them all, at Stourbridge, near Cambridge, ceased in 1927. Those who value the traditions of over 600 years will have to be on their guard.

CHAPTER V

"THE BEAKS"

THE LAW AND FAIRS

The legal position relating to Fairs is, to say the least, complex, and we have identified close on one hundred Acts impinging in some way on Fairgrounds. Because some Fairs have been established by Royal Charter and others have grown up piecemeal as demand arose, and as there have been many changes of fashion in regard to ownership of land, hygiene, public order and decency, and the environment, new problems have been identified and former Acts repealed.

Among the topics dealt with by this legislation are:

The establishment of a Fair possibly harming any neighbouring ones;

Holding of Fairs on Sundays or Saints' Days;

The holding of Fairs on more days or for longer hours than allowed in the original charter or grant;

The power to alter the set days of a Fair or abolish them altogether;

Questions over ownership of the Fair and therefore of tolls arising;

The appointment of a "sufficient person" to take tolls and keep a record;

The overcharging of tolls by the owners of Fairs;

Claims of monopoly of right to sell goods at a Market or Fair;

The prevention of selling on the way to Market, thus avoiding tolls;

Illicit, under-cover trading at a Fair, for the same reason;

The re-selling at a profit of goods already bought at the same Market;

Stolen goods being sold at a Market or Fair;

Below-standard weights and measures being used by traders;

The extent of the jurisdiction of the "pie-powder" courts set up to try offences committed at the time of a Fair;

The safe conduct of merchants bringing produce for sale;

The licensing of itinerant hawkers;

Public health risks from travellers in mobile homes;

The possibility of spreading contagious diseases among animals;

The sale of intoxicating liquor;

Adulteration of food and drink;

The inspection of food preparation to satisfy hygiene requirements;

The disturbance of the peace by noise or riotous behaviour;

The dangers of fire or public safety;

Whether laws applying to Trading Fairs also applied to Pleasure Fairs.

Fair Enough?

It would be inappropriate here to express any opinions about the current legal situation. Legal textbooks, however, maintain that a Fair, strictly speaking, Is the right to hold a gathering of buyers and sellers, and does not really apply to that gathering or the place where it is held. A Fair is a big Market held once or twice a year, whereas a Market occurs possibly every week. The rights to hold a Fair can be forfeited to the Crown if there is an unauthorised change of date or for taking an extortionate amount in tolls.

To prevent people setting up unwarranted Fairs, the Metropolitan Fairs Act of 1868 required the owner of a Fair where none had been held for each of seven previous years to show proof of his right to hold such a Fair.

By the Fairs Act of 1868, which was replaced by a modified version in 1871, the Home Secretary can abolish a Fair at the request of the owner. The 1873 Fairs Act allowed the Home Secretary to approve a change of date for a Fair. Pinner Fair was changed from Whit week to the Wednesday after the Spring Bank Holiday by an Order from the Home Secretary in 1972.

Other regulations, especially in London, like the Metropolitan Police Act of 1839, govern the hours within which a Fair may be held: this ensures that neighbouring houses get some peace after midnight. That Act also gave magistrates the right to ban Fairs with no known owner (see page 105).

The word 'fair' was originally used to describe the pleasurable gatherings on a feast day, usually connected (as at Pinner) with the saint to whom the local church was dedicated. A whole range of Public Health, Gaming and other Acts have tried to define what is meant by a Fair, so that local authorities could make bye-laws regulating the size, duration or behaviour of Fairs and their visitors. The 1961 Public Health Act, for example, concerned with the preservation of public order and safety and the prevention of fire, allows controls over a Pleasure Fair, defined as a place

"which is for the time being used wholly or mainly for providing any entertainment for the admission to which or for the use of any contrivance in which a charge is made, such as circuses, exhibitions of human beings or performing animals; merry-go-rounds, roundabouts, swings, or switchback railways; coconut shies, hoop-la's, shooting galleries or bowling alleys; dodgems or other mechanical riding or driving contrivances; automatic or other machines intended for amusement or entertainment; or anything similar to the fore-going."

Thus the heavy weight of legal draftsmen tries to imagine any possible attempt by cunning showmen to provide some new thrill for the young at heart that might not be covered by the regulations.

One of the earliest Acts dealing with Fairs and Markets was in 1448:

SUNDAY FAIRS ACT 1448 (c.5, 27 Henry VI)

WHEREAS

Considering the abominable injuries and offences done to Almighty God and to his Saints, always aiders and singular assisters in our necessities, because of Fairs and Markets upon the high and principal feasts as in the feast of the Ascension of our Lord, in the day of Corpus Christi, in the day of Whit Sunday, in Trinity Sunday, with other Sundays and also in the high feast of the Assumption of our blessed lady, the day of All Saints, and on Good Friday accustomably and miserably holden and used in the realm of England; in which principal feasts and festival days for great earthly covetise the people is more willingly vexed and in bodily labour foiled *(pro magna cupiditate terrena populus voluntarie plus vexatus et in labore corporali deturbatus existit)* than in other ferial days as in fastening and making their booths and stalls and bearing and carrying, lifting and placing their wares outward and homewards as though they did nothing to remember the horrible defiling of their souls in buying and selling, with many deceitful lies and false perjury, with drunkenness and strifes, and so especially withdrawing themselves and their servants from Divine service,

The King hath ORDAINED

(1) That all manner of Fairs and Markets in the said principal feasts and Sundays and Good Friday shall clearly cease from all shewing of any goods and merchandise (necessary victual only except) upon pain of forfeiture of all goods to the lord of franchise or liberty where such goods be shewed (the four Sundays in harvest excepted).

(2) They which of old time have sufficient days before the feasts aforesaid shall hold their Markets the full number of days except Good Friday and Sundays.

(3) But granteth to them power which of old time had no day to hold their Fair or Market but only upon the festival days aforesaid to hold by the same authority and strength of his old grant within three days next before the said feasts or next after, the proclamation first made to the simple common people.

(To take effect from the Feast of St Michael next.)

(Pickering's *Statutes*)

Fair Enough?

PROTESTS

A Fair occurring once a year, in which the peaceful tenour of village life is abruptly disturbed, is bound to cause some offence, as we have seen. From time to time, people have complained to the authorities and endeavoured to suppress the merry-making or unruly behaviour, as they saw it.

In 1829, for reasons not known, the local magistrates at Edgware tried to ban Pinner Fair. Local farmers banded together to present a petition to the Lord of the Manor, Lord Northwick, begging him to allow it to continue.

The petition was drawn up by John Smart, a professional artist who lived at Chestnut Cottage in Church Lane.

The following is an extract:

My Lord

Several of the most respectable and the oldest inhabitants of this place are much hurt by an imperious and arbitrary order from the Magistrates of Edgware to put down Pinner Fair.

My Lord, you will find it a very ancient Fair. There are several old inhabitants who perfectly well remember this a Cattle Fair and have seen cattle bought and exposed for sale. The Beadle of Harrow has constantly attended in your name and taken a triffle (sic) for tolls for Stalls, Booths etc., and no doubt formerly for cattle: they attended even up to last year[13].

Now may we beg of you, my Lord, as a great favour, if you can give us any information as to our right to hold this Fair, as the old inhabitants whose names I subjoin are determined to defend their public right in every legal way. The Magistrates say that if they succeed with Pinner they will put down Harrow Fair.

Your Lordship's faithful & obdt Servt

John Smart

P.S. I subjoin some of the names that you may judge of the respectability of the application:

Messrs. Ellis of Pinner Marsh, Ewer of Pinner (Gibsons), Hill of Headstone, Thos Hill of Pinner, Charles Laurence of East End, Longbottom of Woodhall, Smart, Benjn Weall of Hatch End, John Weall of Oxy Lane, Benjn Wilshin of Waxwell and a very great proportion of the Inhabitants of the Parish.

[Reprinted by kind permission of the Corporation of London: Greater London Record Office. Accession 76/1804]

(Unfortunately, the Petty Sessions records for this period do not exist, so the reasons for the magistrates' objections are not known. Nor is there a copy of Lord Northwick's reply to Mr Smart, but no action was taken to ban the fair.)

(John Smart had written the previous month to Lord Northwick informing him that he had painted a number of pictures lately and would be honoured to show them to his Lordship.)

13 It is not clear to whom the "they" refers, the Beadles or the cattle

HARROW FAIR: THE FIRST ATTEMPT

Four miles from Pinner, at Harrow on the Hill, an even older Fair took place every year. Its Charter was signed by King Henry III in 1260/1 and was confirmed by Edward II in 1315, to be held at the time of the Nativity of the Virgin Mary, September 7 - 9. As this fell during term time, the Governors of Harrow School had persuaded the authorities to change the date to the first Monday in August, when there would be no schoolboys around to be corrupted. In spite of its retaining a good reputation, however, strong efforts were made in the 19th century to suppress it, and eventually the protesters had their way: this could so easily have been the fate of Pinner Fair.

1837   The Annual Fair on the first Monday in August at Harrow is free from the vice and immorality prevalent at Fairs nearer to the Metropolis. (*Visitors' Companion*, 1837)

1850   The Harrow Fair is remarkably free from scenes of vice and dissipation usually prevalent at Fairs near London, the sports being exclusively of a rural character. (*Smith's Handbook* 1850)

1858   The greatest amount of business done at Harrow Fair was with the juvenile portion of pleasure seekers, what with peep-shows, swing-boats, circuses etc., "Cheap Jack" seemed to drive a good trade with a host of admiring rustics. (*Harrow Gazette* 5th August 1858)

1859   A petition was submitted to Lord Northwick, to abolish Harrow Fair. (A copy was sent also to the Commissioner of the Metropolitan Police, Sir Robert Mayne). It was signed by a hundred of the leading citizens, who objected to the annual Charter Fair still being held there in the streets. The signatories included almost all the staff of Harrow School.

Although it is not dated, the names include the Head Master, Dr. Vaughan, who retired in December 1859, and R B Hayward, who joined the School in January 1859. Presumably it was presented in the Spring or Summer of that year:

We beg to submit to your Lordship's consideration the following facts:

1. That the Fair is of no real benefit to any class of the inhabitants of Harrow.

2. That it is productive of deep and serious injury to the morals of the lower classes by introducing among them an occasion of riot, drunkenness and debauchery of all kinds.

3. That it is the cause of great inconvenience by blocking up the chief thoroughfare in the Village and rendering it even dangerous to drive or ride through the streets.

4. That it is obsolete and unnecessary, suited to a primitive state of society and a small population; but now superseded by good shops, good institutions and more rational means of amusement.

Fair Enough?

5. That the abolition of Greenwich, and other large Fairs in the vicinity of the Metropolis, indicates the healthier tone which is beginning to prevail generally on this subject, in other places.

The undersigned acknowledge and respect the antiquity and high authority of the Charter under which the Harrow Fair is held, but we would fain hope that the Lord of the Manor of Harrow will take so favourable a view of the real interests of the village, as to waive a right, the continued exercise of which would maintain an institution most prejudicial to the sound morals and good order of the population.

From the tone of the petition, one wonders if it had been drawn up by Dr. Vaughan himself. Certainly ten of the first dozen names are from the School. Local householders of note include E F Elliott of The Mount, Captain in the Harrow Rifles, whose daughter Georgina was two years later to marry Dr. Montagu Butler, Vaughan's successor as Head Master. Other notables were Arthur Lang, J P, of Sudbury Hill House, a retired Indian Civil Servant; J C Templer of Dudley Lodge, a Master in the Court of the Exchequer and a Churchwarden at St Mary's; and three other legal luminaries, E P Hathaway of Oak Tree Cottage, Greenhill, a barrister, and Richard Beachcroft and Henry Young, solicitors.

The Vicar, Rev J W Cunningham, supported the abolition, as did his son, and his curates, Rev James Jeakes and Rev R J Knight.

Lending powerful voices were Major-General T C Parr, ex-Indian Army, and George Beauchamp Cole, Deputy Lieutenant for Middlesex. With this kind of support for abolition, Lord Northwick must have felt that he could well do without the income from tolls that the parish Beadle had collected on his behalf until he instructed him not to do so in 1859. The Fair seemed doomed.

Many of these prominent people were honorary members of the Harrow Rifle Club and Managers of the Harrow Savings Bank. Not all were residents of long standing, however; as with many traditional institutions, the opposition came from the growing number of upper-middle class residents in Sudbury and Greenhill rather than from the farming families who had lived in Harrow for several generations. Some of the petitioners had sons at Harrow School and had perhaps moved to Harrow especially to take advantage of the free places still on offer to Harrow residents.

[Corporation of London: Greater London Record Office - Accession 643 2nd Deposit]

ATTEMPT TO SUPPRESS HARROW FAIR

Mr Edward Tarlton, Superintendent of T Division of the Metropolitan Police, applied to the Court (at Edgware) under the direction of the Commissioner, Sir Robert Mayne, for the purpose of asking them to grant a summons against the Lord of the Manor of Harrow for the purpose of bringing his Lordship before the Bench in order that he might show cause why he allows a Fair to be held in Harrow Town on the first Monday in August of each year.

"THE FAIRS ACT, 1871."

HARROW-ON-THE-HILL FAIR,

IN pursuance of the above mentioned Act, I, the Right Honourable Henry Austin Bruce, one of Her Majesty's principal Secretaries of State, hereby notify as follows :—

1.—By memorial dated 29 May, 1872, a representation has been duly made to me by the Justices sitting in Petty Sessions for the division of Gore, in the county of Middlesex, that a Fair has been annually held on the first Monday in the month of August, in the Parish of Harrow-on-the-Hill, in the said division, in the county of Middlesex, and that it would be for the convenience and advantage of the public that such Fair should be abolished.

2.—On the fifth day of July, 1872, I shall take the aforesaid representation into consideration, and all persons are to intimate before that day any objection they may desire to offer to the abolition of the said Fair.

Signed,

H. A. BRUCE.

Whitehall, 5th June, 1872.

The Home Secretary considers abolishing Harrow Fair.

Fair Enough?

The Bench, after a long consultation, declined to interfere, as it could not be shewn that his Lordship was either owner or occupier of the ground on which the Fair is held.

On the 1st of August the Fair was held as usual, but we never remember so few stalls and shows and visitors as on this occasion. For the first time in the memory of man, the Beadle of the parish, in pursuance of orders given him, ceased to collect tolls in the name of the Lord of the Manor.

It appears to be a general opinion that owing to the tolls being relinquished, a much larger number of shows and stalls will congregate next year, unless in the meantime the Fair be suppressed. The usual old English sports of climbing the greasy pole, running in sacks etc., did not take place.

The stalls and shows closed earlier than customary.

(Harrow Gazette, 2nd August 1859)

THE SECOND ATTEMPT

1862   "A Lover of Peace and Quietness" wrote to the *Harrow Gazette*, asking how much longer the nuisance of Harrow Fair was to be tolerated. Why could it not, he asked, be moved to a field outside the town? Footpaths and roadways were blocked, to the equal danger of the pedestrian and the equestrian. He complained also about damage to the "excellent road". (1st September 1862)

1866   "The Anniversary will soon arrive......of this annual infliction of blackguardism (Harrow Fair). We have no desire to deprive the poor of their accustomed holiday....but the sooner it is put down the better. The metal of our roads is invariably disturbed and our water and gas pipes run a great risk of being injured." (*Harrow Gazette* 1st June 1866)

"Harrow Fair has again been held to the detriment of our roads and footpaths and injury to the morals of our poorer brethren. No doubt much money is ill-spent at our Fair by children and parents who can ill afford it." (*Harrow Gazette* 1st September 1866)

1867   "Harrow Fair showed a marked improvement, with stalls down one side of the street only, giving more convenience to conveyances passing through." Among the stalls were rifle galleries and butchers with hot sausages, together with "a variety of other amusements so prevalent at country fairs."(*Harrow Gazette* 2nd September 1867)

1868   The Fairs Act (replaced in 1871) allowed for the suppression of Fairs in streets (see the poem on page 8).

1870   In January, the Superintendent of the local Police summoned Lord Northwick under an Act of 1839 to prove his right to hold a Fair. As in 1859, the magistrate said he was neither the occupier nor the owner of the land on which the Fair was held, that is the Harrow High Street. (*Harrow Gazette* 29th January 1870)

CHAP. 12.

An Act to further amend the Law relating to Fairs in England and Wales. [25th May 1871.]

WHEREAS certain of the fairs held in England and Wales are unnecessary, are the cause of grievous immorality, and are very injurious to the inhabitants of the towns in which such fairs are held, and it is therefore expedient to make provision to facilitate the abolition of such fairs:

Be it enacted by the Queen's most Excellent Majesty, by and with the advice and consent of the Lords Spiritual and Temporal, and Commons, in this present Parliament assembled, and by the authority of the same, as follows:

Title.
1. This Act may be cited as "The Fairs Act, 1871."

Definition of "owner."
2. In this Act the term "owner" means any person or persons, or body of commissioners, or body corporate, entitled to hold any fair, whether in respect of the ownership of any lands or tenements, or under any charter, letters patent, or Act of Parliament, or otherwise howsoever.

Secretary of State may, on representation of magistrates, with consent of owner, order fair to be abolished.
3. In case it shall appear to the Secretary of State for the Home Department, upon representation duly made to him by the magistrates of any petty sessional district within which any fair is held, or by the owner of any fair in England or Wales, that it would be for the convenience and advantage of the public that any such fair shall be abolished, it shall be lawful for the said Secretary of State for the Home Department, with the previous consent in writing of the owner for the time being of such fair, or of the tolls or dues payable in respect thereof, to order that such fair shall be abolished accordingly:

An extract from the Fairs Act 1871 as published in the local paper.

THE FAIRS ACT, 1871.

HARROW-ON-THE-HILL FAIR, MIDDLESEX.

WHEREAS a representation has been duly made to me as Secretary of State for the Home Department by the Justices sitting in Petty Sessions, for the Division of Gore, in the County of Middlesex, that a Fair has been annually held on the first Monday in the month of August, in the Parish of Harrow-on-the-Hill, in the said Division of the said County, and that it would be for the convenience and advantage of the public that the said Fair should be abolished.

AND WHEREAS notice of the said representation and of the time when I should take the same into consideration has been duly published in pursuance of "the Fairs Act, 1871."

AND WHEREAS on such representation and consideration, it appears to me that it would be for the convenience and advantage of the public that the said Fair should be abolished.

AND WHEREAS it appears that there is no Lord or owner of the said Fair and the tolls thereof,

NOW THEREFORE I, as the Secretary of State for the Home Department, in exercise of the powers vested in me by the Fairs Act, 1871, DO HEREBY ORDER that the Fair which has been annually held on the first Monday in the month of August, in the parish of Harrow-on-the-Hill, in the Petty Sessional Division of Gore, in the County of Middlesex, shall be abolished as from the date of this Order.

Given under my Hand, at Whitehall,
    this 12th day of July, 1872.

Signed,
H. A. BRUCE.

The Home Secretary abolished Harrow Fair 1872

The Annual Fair at Harrow on August 1st had many stalls including one run by Mrs Bragg, who had been coming for 50 years to the same site. There was considerable uproar until late in the evening, but the police were not troubled. The School had broken up a week earlier.(*Harrow Gazette* 13th August 1870)

1871 "It is time Harrow Fair is either abolished or moved to a field. Every inch of the ground on which the stalls are fixed is part of a highway and it is clearly illegal for the owners of the stalls to obstruct any portion of the highway to the danger of the public. ...The Fair, still preserving its mediaeval absurdities, is neither amusing nor instructive, and tends to deprave the taste of the people. Why not substitute an annual fête in its place in the School Field at Greenhill?" (Letter from "Progress" in *Harrow Gazette* 12th August 1871)

Another Fairs Act was passed, replacing the 1868 one, and giving the Home Secretary the power to abolish a Fair "if it was thought to be unnecessary or injurious to the public or its abolition would be for the convenience and advantage of the public." Representations had to be made to him by the local magistrates (by the local councils after 1894). Even Charter Fairs were not exempt. The following year, some seventy Fairs were abolished, among them Harrow and Watford.

1872 In May, the magistrates in Petty Sessions at Edgware applied for an Order for the abolition of Harrow Fair, as this annual event held on the first Monday in August was felt to be to the detriment of the morals of the neighbourhood. There appeared to be no owner of the Fair. Austin Bruce, the Home Secretary (Lord Aberdare) made the Order, and Harrow Fair was abolished on 12th July under the 1871 Act. It was strange that Lord Northwick did not claim ownership, as his widow did for Pinner twenty years later.

In June, "A Tradesman" wrote to the paper regretting the departure of the Fair, as trade had always been brisker on the day it was held. He hoped some way would be found of giving the tradesmen the benefit of customers and of giving "the poor man and his children" a holiday.

"A Well-wisher to the Poor" replied that he hailed with satisfaction the abolition of the Fair as the showmen had made holes in the road with crowbars, as well as for other nuisances not to be mentioned. The fire-plugs (hydrants) were covered with stalls. Many visitors were from London and not of the best character. "It is time the mediaeval tom-foolery of our Fairs was done away with. Harrow being a one-day Fair, only the commonest description of shows and stalls ever visit the town. It has never answered the purpose of the owners of the larger stalls to attend it; besides if they did there would not be space enough for them." Only the publicans, he said, would suffer by the abolition. (*Harrow Gazette* 15th June 1872)

[Information File, Harrow Reference Library]

Fair Enough?
FURTHER PROTESTS & COMMENTS ON PINNER AND OTHER FAIRS

1838   The Enfield magistrates were asked by the showmen to grant an extra day for the Fair there as it had been spoilt by torrential rain. The magistrates thought the showmen were vagabonds and moved them on.

1846   "Fairs within half an hour's journey of London which are still held are in a state of visible decadence." (Gregory, a showman)

1860: "Representation having been made to the Ely Local Board of Health that the Fairs held in the City of Ely by virtue of ancient Charters are the sources of much evil to the inhabitants and neighbourhood, it was resolved by the Board that it is expedient that power should be entrusted to some local authority to regulate the same and also to limit their duration. And it appearing that while the Local Government Act of 1858 provides for the regulation of Markets by Local Boards and incorporates therewith the provisions of the Markets & Fairs Clauses Act of 1847 so far as relates to Markets, yet the said Act is wholly silent as to Fairs.

"Resolved further, that it is expedient that the powers now vested in Local Boards for the regulation of existing Markets should also be extended to Fairs and that further powers should be conferred on Local Boards as well as to shorten the duration of such Fairs, as also to make bye-laws for prescribing the hours during which such Fairs should be open and for regulating and controlling the various exhibitions, performances and entertainments thereat; and that such powers should be conferred by a general measure emanating from the Government, rather than by the expensive process of separate measures originating from each locality". (*Harrow Gazette* 1st June 1860)

1870   "The people about here can run up to London and back for a shilling any day in the week, all the year round, and see all the living curiosities in the Zoo, and the stuffed ones in the Museum and go in the evening to a theatre or music-hall. They have no need of Fairs. (Croydon resident)

1872   In November the Watford magistrates, supported by sixty prominent citizens in a "numerously and respectably signed memorial", applied for a ban on their two Fairs, one on the second Tuesday after Whitsun and the other a Hiring Fair on 8-9 September. They pointed out that servants were no longer hired at the Fair, that entertainments were better provided at Crystal Palace, then easily reached by train, and that the shows demoralized and degraded the young people for whom they were intended. The owner, the Earl of Essex, agreed and the Fairs were abolished on 30th December 1872. (Public Record Office HO45/9321/17169)

1873   A visitor to Kingston Fair on a sunny Saturday morning found that there were few people around, the gingerbread sellers were weary, the swings and roundabouts idle, the creatures in the menagerie listless and only the feeble clack of cymbals broke the silence. (Frost 1874 : see Bibliography)

1874 "Fairs are becoming extinct because with the progress of the nation they have ceased to possess any value in the social economy either as marts of trade or a means of popular amusement. All the large towns now possess music halls and many have a theatre. The last showman will soon be as great a curiosity as the dodo. The Nation has outgrown Fairs, which are as dead as the generations which they have delighted." (Frost 1874, Pp376 - 377)

"Pinner Fair has degenerated into an insignificant Pleasure Fair held annually on Whit Monday[14]. (Walford, *Greater London*)

1880 The noise of steam roundabouts at a Fair at Willesden was said to be liable to "drive people to lunacy." (Public Record Office MEPO/2/374)

1881 Pinner Fair is said to be "played out", but the amusements "have not quite lost their charm." Thanks to the tact of the Police Inspector "the day passed off without the public peace being disturbed in any way." (*Watford Observer* 9th July 1881).

1883 The Trustees for the owners of a field in Edgware applied to the Home Office to ban the annual Fair there. Originally for the sale of cattle on two days and for pleasure on the third, it had become merely a three-day entertainment. They wanted the land for housing near the new Edgware station. If they were not allowed to do this, they threatened to increase the rents for pitches, which would cause disturbance and lead possibly to a riot. This persuasive argument was counter-balanced by a petition from local tradesmen and cottagers. There was no other form of entertainment locally for young or old. The police concurred that there had never been any charges arising from the Fair over the past twenty years, and that it was well conducted. The Home Secretary, Sir William Vernon-Harcourt, saw no reason to ban the Fair, and it took place again in August. In November, another petition was organised against it, signed by local clergy and publicans in an unholy alliance; once again the Home Office saw no reason to comply. (Information from Crown Copyright material in the Public Record Office, Ref. HO 45/9635/A28972)

1884 Sir William Vernon-Harcourt, the Home Secretary, issued an edict to the police, stating that no attempt should be made to interfere with "the innocent amusements of the poorer classes." This was quoted by the police in many of their responses to complaints about Fairs over the next fifty years. [Public Record Office MEPO/2/5092]

1886 In the trial at the Old Bailey of John Studt, for playing music in Stoke Newington in a public place of entertainment without a licence, he was charged under an Act of 1751. He had rented a plot of land and held a Fair there, and it was alleged by the local council that the noise of the steam organs and the "tumult caused by the persons assembled there was a nuisance to the

14 'An error for 'Wednesday'

Fair Enough?

neighbourhood." Such entertainment, it was said, might be harmless in a country district once a year but was unsuitable for the centre of the metropolis. Arguments raged as to whether the music was an essential part of a roundabout or merely to attract people to it. The police claimed that the Fair was an advantage to the neighbourhood, as it attracted the rough juvenile element from the streets, which were thus made quieter. Studt was found guilty and the Fair was closed. (*The Times* 21st January 1886)

1887. Formation of the United Kingdom Showmen & Van Dwellers Association (which became the Showmen's Guild by 1910) in answer to a Bill in Parliament which aimed to license live-in caravans.

1889 Lord Northwick, the 3rd Baron and Lord of the Manor, died on November 18th.

THE EVENTS OF 1893-4 REGARDING PINNER FAIR

In December 1893, Mr Loveland-Loveland, Deputy Chairman of Middlesex Quarter Sessions and living at Barrow Point House, in association with Thomas Blackwell of The Cedars, Harrow Weald, and a Mr Hill[15] submitted a petition to the Lady of the Manor of Harrow (the widowed Lady Northwick) and to the magistrates[16] at the Petty Sessions at Edgware. Lady Northwick agreed to their request to abolish Pinner Fair and as the rightful owner signed an agreement to do so.

The petition was presented to the magistrates on January 10th 1894, by Mr Hill in the absence of Mr Loveland-Loveland. He said the Fair had become a nuisance, no cattle being offered for sale, it merely being an excuse for rioting and drunkenness. On the Fair day, he complained, there was hardly room for a cart to pass down the street. "The people who attended mostly came from London and were a great nuisance to the inhabitants."

Lady Northwick supported the petition even more strongly. Not only was the road impassable but "many undesirable people came from Whitechapel." She also claimed that the Fair had been known to bring disease into the district, though no evidence for this was offered.

After a long debate, the magistrates decided by three to one to send the petition on to Mr Asquith, the Home Secretary. *The London Gazette* and local papers carried an official announcement the following week that the petition had been received and representations were to be sent to the Home Office by February 17th.

A week later, Thomas Barnes, the shoemaker at the bottom of the High Street, wrote to Mr Asquith protesting at the proposal. A counter-petition was drawn up and signed by two hundred people. It was presented to the Edgware Bench by Daniel Soames[17] a solicitor on 24th January, though the Ellement family claimed later that it had been organised by Thomas Ellement, builder of The Oddfellows Arms, and his son George Cornelius. This petition showed that the Fair had been in existence for over 500 years, that large sums of money were spent annually among the shopkeepers of the village, and that no serious charges of drunkenness had ever been made, and indeed in most years no charges of any kind. They claimed further that sales of cattle and farm implements still occasionally took place. The great bulk of the inhabitants, they said, were in favour of the Fair.

Some debate took place about the size of the High Street, Mr Hill claiming it was only 24 feet wide and Mr Soames pointing out that it was 60 feet wide at the foot and 90 feet at the top[18]. Mr Soames' petition was supported by 35 people whose frontages faced onto the site of the Fair.

On the advice of W S Gilbert and his fellow magistrates, Mr Soames sent his counter-petition on to the Home Secretary and all the claims were considered. The Home Office asked the police to report on the conduct of visitors to the Fair or whether "the abolition would interfere with the reasonable enjoyment of any class of people", and after some prompting they eventually replied. Evidently they did not agree that it "was attended by disorder and immorality."

On 2nd May 1894, Mr Leigh-Pemberton of the Home Office wrote to all those who had corresponded and informed them that "after careful consideration of all the facts, the conduct of those frequenting it and the local inconvenience caused," he was not satisfied that it would be for the public advantage to abolish the Fair and that he therefore declined to make the requested Order.

Legend has it that Mr Asquith visited the Fair to see for himself before making his decision; but the Fair that year was not held until 16th May. In any case Mr Asquith was married on 1st May to Margot Tennant and would have been far too pre-occupied.

It is also suggested by Ware and in *The Villager* 113 that the magistrates deferred their decision as they knew that their powers in this case were shortly to be handed over to the newly formed Hendon Urban District Council. The newspaper reports show that the petition was sent the day it was received.

---

15 There is some mystery about the identity of Mr Hill. In newspaper reports he is called John Hill, though there was no-one of that name in the 1891 Census for Pinner. In the course of his arguments he stated that in 1893 he had penned animals in the High Street outside his house and that these had been removed by the showmen. This would seem to refer to Daniel Hill of Church Farm, the wealthy bachelor farmer who had tried to divert the Fair in 1868 by offering a field (see page 8) and who in 1897 planted trees on the sites used by showmen (see page 82).

16 The magistrates on January 10th 1893 were Mr Helsham-Jones of Pinner Hill (Chairman), Mr J M Garrard, the London Crown Jeweller who lived at Pinner Place, Mr Nelson, and the septuagenarian Dr Thomas Bridgwater of Harrow, who had been one of the signatories of the 1859 petition protesting against Harrow Fair.

17 Daniel Robert Soames, born 1849, solicitor, son of Daniel Wilshin Soames of The Lodge. In 1894 he was living in Kilburn High Road.

18 Both were right. The Fair was then allowed only on the road and not the pavements. Between kerbs opposite what is now Barter's Walk the road is 26' wide. It widens out at the junction with Bridge Street and of course considerably at the top, so Mr Soames' figures also applied: a good example of the manipulation of statistics.

In the matter of The Fairs Act
1871 ——— and ———

In the matter of the proposed
abolition of a Fair accustomed to be held
in the hamlet of Pinner and parish of
Harrow in the County of Middlesex. ———

I The Right Honorable Elizabeth
Augusta Lady Northwick of
Northwick Park in the County of Worcester being
the Lady of the Manors of Harrow and Pinner
now known as one Manor and usually called
the Manor of Harrow and as such the Owner
of the above-mentioned Fair within the meaning
of the above-mentioned Statute Do hereby
consent to the abolition of the said Fair
Dated this fifteenth day of December
One thousand eight hundred and ninety three

Elizabeth Augusta Northwick

Certificate from Lady Northwick authorising the closure of Pinner Fair 1893

THE FAIRS ACT, 1871.

PINNER FAIR.

IN pursuance of the above-mentioned Act, I, the Right Honourable Herbert Henry Asquith, one of Her Majesty's principal Secretaries of State, hereby notify as follows :—

1. By Memorial dated the 10th day of January 1894, a representation has been duly made to me by the Justices of the Petty Sessional Division of Gore, in the County of Middlesex, that a Fair has been annually held in Whitsun-Wednesday, in the Hamlet of Pinner, in the Parish of Harrow, in the said Division of the said County, and that it would be for the convenience and advantage of the public that such Fair should be abolished :

2. On the 17th day of February, 1894, I shall take the aforesaid representation into consideration, and all persons are to intimate before that day any objection they may desire to offer to the abolition of the said Fair.

(Signed,)

Whitehall,   H. H. ASQUITH.
    17th January, 1894.

Mr Asquith consults local opinion

Fair Enough?

Mr Soames expressed his thanks for the reprieve, saying that it met the wishes of 19 out of 20 of the inhabitants.

Attendances at Pinner Fair were said to have increased every year after this attempt to stop it. A poster was produced for the Fair that year modelled on the earlier ones of 1831-41, even using the same printer. It suggested that buying and selling of cattle would take place "according to ancient custom."

This was possibly an attempt to persuade the authorities that this was more than just a Pleasure Fair. (Though Tom Ellement did claim that in his father's and grandfather's days it was a Cattle and Hiring Fair, there is little other evidence as yet for this.)

[Information from local papers and from Crown Copyright material in the Public Record Office classes HO 43/185-6, HO 45/B15620 by permission of H M S O]

PINNER FAIR.

According to Ancient Custom founded upon a Charter granted to the Lord of the Manor and Inhabitants by King Edward the 3rd, in the 10th year of his reign, 1337,

A Fair will be held at Pinner

FOR THE

BUYING & SELLING

OF

CATTLE & MERCHANDISE

On WHITSUN WEDNESDAY, the 16th of May, 1894.

PEACOCK, PRINTER, WATFORD.

LATER COMMENTS AND PROTESTS HERE AND ELSEWHERE

1895 Littlehampton UDC asked the Home Secretary to abolish their May Fair as the streets were obstructed, causing a nuisance. The occupants of Surrey Street, where the Fair was held, petitioned for it to be retained. (Frances Brown, *op.cit.*)

1896 *The Harrow Gazette* asked, "Why should the jolly people of Pinner, who, we take it, are in the majority, forfeit their right to one day's giddy frivolity out of a possible 365? Let Fairs continue. It gives us pleasure to see the merry faces of the lads and lasses on this occasion." (30th May 1896)

1897 Middlesex County Council bye-law restraining noise from shooting galleries, roundabouts and organs. Trees in Pinner High Street uprooted by showmen.

1899 Bognor, Sussex, tried to ban their five-day Fair because of the "hideous noise", but the Fair was held on private ground over which the council had no control.

(Objections were raised in a number of towns by newly-elected Committees of Sanitation, Health or Housing. Bye-laws at Chichester forbade the playing of steam organs on roads, and prohibited swing-boats, shooting galleries and roundabouts on public streets.)

1900 No objection was raised at the Littlehampton Fair on 26th May 1900 as the people were celebrating the Relief of Mafeking on the 17th.(Brown *op.cit*)

1901 "The Pinner Fair is clearly on the decline." *(Harrow Gazette*, 31st May)

1903 "Though often threatened with destruction, Pinner Fair continues to flourish." Mr Eck, Chairman of the Hendon RDC, thought there was no advantage to be gained by having a Fair at Pinner which seemed to be pretty full of people from Watford and district. Mr G C Ellement replied that this showed how popular it was or they would not have come: "In Pinner everyone wanted the Fair."

Mr Toovey, of Church Lane, pointed out that "flying horses" had obstructed the footpath, and were a source of danger. He was advised to take out a summons, which he said he would do, to open up the whole question of the Fair. (*Harrow Observer* 5th June)

It was about this time that Hendon RDC tried to ban Pinner Fair on the grounds that there was no Charter extant. Edwin Ware searched the Public Record Office for a week, and with the help of its former Assistant Keeper, Dr. James Gairdner of Nower Hill, he managed to trace it and have it photographed. Dr. Gairdner died in 1912 aged 84.

1904 Chichester Council attempted to ban their October Sloe Fair: the Board of Guardians wanted to use the Fair field for a workhouse extension. The Salvation Army were preaching strongly against intemperance on these occasions. The authorities were unsuccessful and the following year the crowds were bigger than ever.(Brown *op.cit*)

Fair Enough?

1906 "Every year the village of Pinner has a tussle with the Progressives who think such frivolity unbecoming to the dignity of a rising town that has long ceased to be a chapelry of Harrow, and whose days as a village are numbered." (*The Sunday People*)

1907 At Stockton-on-Tees, the Council wanted to abolish the 700-year-old Charter Fair in the streets. "In these days of progress and reform, experience has taught the fact that age alone does not justify the existence of rights and customs," they declared. "During the last fifty years, in keeping with the strides of inventive genius, the number and proportion of Fair attractions have increased enormously." (*World's Fair* 1st June)

Mitcham Conservators tried to close the Common to showmen, but 600 arrived and took it over.

1908 "There would appear to be an entire cessation to the hostilities aroused by the annual Whitsun Fair in Pinner." (*Harrow Gazette* 12th June)

1909 The Middlesex County Council passed a bye-law "For Good Rule and Government" on 28th October (see page 124).

1910 "If the enthusiastic objectors to Pinner Fair who carried on a futile agitation to abolish this annual function a few years back had been present, they would have found it never so extensively patronised." (*Harrow Gazette* 20th May)

Hambledon D C appealed to the Home Secretary to ban Haslemere Charter Fair as no cattle had been sold since 1903. The Pleasure Fair had been moved from the streets to the Common in 1905 but when pressurised the showmen threatened to move back to the High Street so the closure was applied for. (Brown *op.cit.*)

1911 "Pinner Fair continues to flourish in spite of an element of criticism which during the past few years has been raised by newcomers. The townspeople have not much to complain of." (*Harrow Gazette* 9th June)

1913 Suffragettes in Devon drew attention to their cause by burning the machines at a Pleasure Fair belonging to a Mr Hancock.

1914 Pinner Fair thought to be doomed because of the war: showmen's horses and traction engines requisitioned, "This is the last year of Pinner Fair." (*Daily Mirror* 3rd June)

1920 Letters to the local paper were sparked off by an anonymous correspondent in May who dreaded the approach of the Fair "with all its attendant evils. ... Once more the village street will be given over to pandemonium and become the happy hunting ground for all the thieves and ruffians in a twenty-mile radius. It is a hot-bed of disease and immorality... and as far as I can see it has no desirable feature whatsoever." If it was necessary to retain a priceless heritage, he suggested moving the Fair to a field and polling the inhabitants of the village to see if they wanted the Fair abolished. (*Harrow Observer*, 24th May)

One writer said he did not weep when the monster roundabout a few yards from his house stopped inflicting its torture on him, but he was prepared to suffer for a day for the convenience and pleasure of others. George C Ellement said his father had collected tolls from the Fair as Parish Constable. "Is it not better," he asked, "to have the Fair in a well-lighted public street than in a field which is unlighted, a private ground and insufficiently police patrolled?"

The Fair, he claimed, was an institution for which the majority of the older inhabitants of Pinner had an affection. Those who did not like it could always keep away from it.

The Editor said the Fair found favour with young and old alike and was welcomed rather than dreaded by those who lived on its line of route. It offered the opportunity for a harmless revel to thousands of people. (ib. 28th May).

1921 "The usual objections were raised, but Pinner Fair was stronger than ever." (*Harrow Observer*, 20th May)

1923 "Many residents grumbled at what they probably thought was rowdiness; some might have spoken of "hooliganism", but on the whole Pinner people recognise that the Fair must come as surely as Whitsuntide and that after all it comes but once a year." (*Harrow Observer*, 25th May)

1925 "Pinner Fair has outlived its useful purpose. but the Fair had a larger number of visitors than ever. The people of Pinner look upon their Fair as a heritage not to be despised." (*Harrow Observer*, 5th June)

1926 Following complaints of undue noise from roundabouts at a Fair in Sudbury, the police found that the music was neither loud nor continuous, that it was not a nuisance, that the showmen had made some attempt at muffling and that the Fair had been coming to the area for far longer than any of the residents had lived nearby. (Public Record Office MEPO/2/5090)

1930 "There has been no further attempt to stop Pinner Fair since the occasion some years ago, though some new tradesmen think it affects their trade." (*Harrow Observer*, 6th June).

After complaints about the noise of a Fair at the Swan & Bottle, Uxbridge, by residents living a quarter of a mile away, the police said the Fair was not a nuisance and was "well patronised by the majority of the poorer classes." (P R O MEPO/2/5090)

1934 Pinner formed part of the new local government area of Harrow, and it was thought likely that the Council would abolish the Fair as had been done in 1872.

Residents in Lordship Lane, Tottenham, complained about "the really outstanding noise" and about gambling at a Fair there. The police repeated the Home Secretary's edict of 1884; but the Home Office commented that the police could act if "undesirables" congregated, in which case the entertainment could not be deemed "innocent pleasure". (P R O MEPO/2/5090)

Fair Enough?

1935   Because of growing traffic congestion, the new Harrow Council tried to introduce a Parliamentary Bill allowing them to draft a bye-law banning Pinner Fair, but the move was defeated.

1936   Residents of Welling, in Kent, complained of a Fair's "nerve-racking noise, ungodly dins and disturbance of children's sleep". They also maintained that a ditch had been used as a convenience and that there was a stench from it for months after the Fair. The proprietor of a "Roll-em-down" stall was fined £1 for gaming. (P R O MEPO/2/5090)

The Standing Joint Committee of the Metropolitan Borough Councils suggested Fairs should be licensed by Borough Councils as this would give them a power of veto because of "nuisance from noise, vibration, smoke, apparatus or music" and to enable them to control sanitary arrangements, traffic flows and the disposal of rubbish. (*The Times,* 6th January)

1939   "There has been talk at intervals of efforts to end this event, but I doubt if it has been much more than talk. The local people like it: not many places can claim a Fair that is 600 years old." (*Harrow Observer,* 2nd June)

"Pinner Fair is one of the most popular in the country. With the tempo caused by modern conditions, a Fair acts as a wonderful safety valve and is a great antidote to the many "isms" which are so prevalent in other countries. There is always a small minority who wish to do away with something, and the abolition of Pinner Fair, like that of so many other Fairs, has often been aimed at by them; the majority, however, want the Fair.

"Fairs have been and still are a great source of amusement to countless thousands of people: in fact they are more popular today than ever. Pinner Fair no doubt found its origin through the Church, whose Bishop knew the value of providing relaxation for his people after a strenuous period of labour. Although the Fair lasts but one day it provides fun and amusement for many thousands of people. Once each year the prosaic Bridge Street is turned into Laughtermakers' Lane. May it always be so." (*The Villager 4,* April)

1941   "Should Pinner Fair Be Abolished? He would be a bold and rash man indeed who dared to suggest the abolition of Pinner's ancient Fair in view of the heated opposition evoked at the recent General Meeting of the Pinner Association by the comparatively mild proposition that the Fair should be suspended 'for the duration'. There is a popular misconception that Pinner Fair is a privilege of the showmen, and that for a brief period they have an absolute right to invade Pinner streets and to use them for their own purposes and profit; and as a consequence that they have the right to determine whether or not the Fair should be held, or at any rate to have a voice in the matter.

"It is true that the showmen are entitled to decide for themselves that they will not attend the Fair, and if they did unanimously so decide there would obviously be very little 'Fair' left. (But) there is nothing in the Charter to support the view that the showmen have any right to determine whether or not the Fair be held.

"The grant of the right to hold a Fair or Market was an exclusive privilege given to an individual or body corporate, who was entitled to demand tolls from the persons who sell in the Market. The Pleasure Fair was originally a mere adjunct to the Business Fair, tolerated by the owner of the Fair as an additional source of revenue....and encouraged as an attraction for buyers with an idle hour or so to pass after the serious business had been despatched." (*The Villager 13*,October 1941)

1942   "In 1893 certain well- (or ill-) disposed persons endeavoured to secure the abolition of Pinner Fair by requesting the local magistrates to take action under the Fairs Act of 1871. The local justices made some demur to entertaining the question of abolishing Pinner Fair, no doubt because the Local Government Act of 1894 had been before Parliament and was ready to receive the Royal Assent. By that Act, the powers and duties of the justices were transferred to the new District Councils. Any future would-be abolitionist must therefore first address himself to the Harrow Urban District Council. There remained the question of who is the owner whose consent is to be obtained. The Charter of 1336 granted the Fair to the then Archbishop of Canterbury; whether the right remains with his successors or whether it has been transferred to the Ecclesiastical Commissioners or otherwise dealt with, is a matter that can be enquired into by anyone anxious to promote "the convenience and advantage of the public" (to quote the 1871 Act) by abolishing the Fair." (*The Villager 14*, February 1942).

1943   "Many of the new inhabitants were superior about our local annual Fair. It was a disgrace, a rabble and they would like The Authorities to stop it. I was very fond of the Fair and happily there was a Charter that The Authorities could not get over by which it had the right to plant itself on us on Wednesday in Whit-week. It had done so for many centuries.... Far, indeed, this Fair had travelled from the days when it had a purpose, when the chapmen came with things to sell that were necessary and could not be obtained elsewhere. Now it was just a riot of noisy amusement, vulgar and irrational, yet somehow stimulating too, both for the continuity of its tradition and for its challenge to the view that there's little to do in life save go to the office.

"I do not know whether Pinner has kept its Fair going in these war years. I should think not. No connoisseur of such occasions went to the Fair till night had come and the lights were up; and such a blaze of light as that would be a strange phenomenon in these darkened days. May it blaze forth again when peace comes.

There's much that I would preserve, and notably any custom that has maintained unbroken tradition, anything which has kept the breath of life, even though it be a raucous and alcoholic breath like that of Pinner Fair." (Howard Spring, *The Villager 17*, February 1943).

117

Fair Enough?

1947 "We have not heard lately of any movement to secure its abolition." (*Harrow Observer*, 5th June)

1950 "A small minority want the Fair abolished. For three years our Whit Monday peace has been disturbed by motor engines, shouting, dogs barking and men throwing poles down from the tops of waggons. Originally, the showmen were not allowed in until 4 p.m. on the Tuesday but concessions were allowed in wartime when the men were quiet and well behaved. Now we have three nights and 2½ days of disturbance, which is not good enough." (Letter to Council, 1st June 1950)

"The crush of people at the foot of the High Street was so great that panic ensued and people had to leap into the Pinn to escape being squashed in the melee." (*Harrow Observer*, 8th June)

"The Fair may be regarded as Pinner's greatest pride or its greatest pest, according to the way you look at it. Peace or war it has carried on just the same and nobody has found a legal way of stopping it." (C A Lejeune, in *The Villager 38*, July 1950)

1952 The Showmen's Guild expressed concern to Middlesex County Planning Department that Harrow UDC intended to restrict Pinner Fair in their Development Plan under the Town & Country Planning Act 1947. The HUDC replied that they could not foresee that they would ever object to the holding of the Fair on planning or any other grounds as it was founded by Royal Charter. (File in Harrow Borough Engineer's Dept)

The local Chamber of Trade asked Harrow UDC to remind police to exercise their powers to restrain the showmen from premature entry into the village (ib.)

1954 One showman had covered the War Memorial with his tent and had used the steps to prop up his frames. This was corrected in 1955. (*Harrow Observer*, 17th June)

1956 The local Chamber of Trade objected to the "fortune hunters" who travelled in the wake of the Fair. The police replied that they thought it unfair to ban itinerant sellers of balloons and paper hats. The Chamber claimed that there was noise from dawn on Monday to dawn on Thursday. The police replied that most of the showmen were at Hampstead Heath on the Monday until 11 p.m. and that no erecting took place until 5 p.m. on Tuesday. Booths were assembled on the road and there was room for the police to walk behind. The showmen, they said, did their best to lessen the annoyance. The Chamber complained that some shopkeepers could not gain access to their premises. The police replied that some shops let their private forecourts to the showmen, and the police had no control over these. They said the Fair must inevitably cause a measure of annoyance. (Engineering Dept. file)

1957 In answer to a query, the police authority pointed out that they had no jurisdiction over the allocation of spaces. The men put down poles and any disputes were sorted out by the Guild. There were no known limits to the Fair. (ib.)

1958 The Council met members of the Showmen's Guild and agreed that no caravans would be allowed within 5 miles of Pinner before 5 a.m.. on the Tuesday. Possible assembly points were suggested and the showmen agreed not to remove any paving stones or excavate beneath them. (ib.)

1959 The Chamber of Trade asked the Council to control the extent of the Fair and to allocate spaces to restrict the signs of uncontrolled expansion. The Council were to enquire of other areas as to their procedure. A charity stall found the showmen unhelpful and there were rumours of a nude display in one of the booths.(ib.)

Mr Owen Faulkner, whose jewellery shop was in Marsh Road beyond the railway bridge, said,"I think the new ruling is a jolly good thing. The Fair has crept beyond the bridge over the past eight years or so and honestly it is just like bedlam. They can't wait for you to shut up shop before they are putting up their stalls, and when they are up they are only a matter of feet away from your front window."

Mr C G Ellement, however, was most vehement in his opposition to these remarks. "The Fair should be left alone," he said. "This is the thin end of the wedge, because we know there are those who would like to get rid of the Fair altogether. This decision should have been left to Pinner people and not to people it has nothing to do with."

Mr Ellement's words were echoed by Mr Beckley, landlord of the Red Lion. "Pinner Fair is the kiddies' day," he said. "For weeks beforehand they save up their pocket money. It should be left as it is. What sort of people are they who can object to the Fair when it is only held for one day? The showmen are some of the nicest and most generous of people."

A lady of 78, who had grown up with the Fair and known it all her life maintained that not all the showmen were now Fair people but just street vendors who came and put their cases down in the middle of the Fair to sell their goods. "I don't mind the caravans," she added. "They are not there long enough outside my window to be worth complaining about." (*Harrow Observer*, 19th November)

1960 The Round Table were concerned about press reports of the Council's intent to control the Fair within stated boundaries which could affect the positioning of their stall. The Council decided to restrict the Fair to High Street and Bridge Street as far as the railway bridge and to assume responsibility for allocation of spaces, as from 1961. Vehicles were not to park outside private houses. This action was in co-operation with the police and the Showmen's Guild. "We hope this is not a step towards doing away with the Fair altogether." (*The Villager 66*, March 1960)

Fair Enough?

1961   Some space was allowed south of the bridge in Marsh Road for generators. Coloured routes were allocated to guide showmen to their sites. One stall-holder, whose family had been coming to the Fair for three generations, forcibly objected to someone else occupying his traditional site. He was arrested but given a conditional discharge. (*Harrow Observer*, June 1961)

1965   A letter to the local press, from Mr Jennery, asked if Pinner really wanted a Fair. Formerly, he said, it was for the sale of essential commodities; nowadays Pinner was besieged by gipsies, who lived in luxury caravans, with ultra-modern appliances and "spotless nylon curtains." Healthy manly sports had been replaced by games of chance like Bingo. There was a "cacophany of noise and an unwarrantable intrusion of privacy." He urged residents to take "staves, pickstaffs, cutlasses and muskets" and repel the invaders. Mr Rathbone of Cuckoo Hill replied. He said he too disliked the smell of hamburgers but "it would be churlish to deny pleasure to thousands of people. For once the smug hideousness of Bridge Street is disguised." (*Harrow Observer*, 3rd June)

1967   It was suggested that Pinner Fair be moved to the Wednesday after the Spring Bank Holiday as numbers fell when children were still at school on Fair day. Showmen now had to apply for a permit. (*Harrow Observer*, 25th May)

1971   As the last Lady of the Manor had died in 1964, the Council were considering purchasing the lordship of the Manor to obtain ownership of the Fair. But there was legal doubt as to who in fact owned the Fair and whether the right to hold a Fair was transferred with the Manor in 1547. As the two Fairs of five days in all were no longer held, it was thought that the Charter was perhaps no longer valid.

[The question seems fairly comprehensively answered by Druett (*Pinner Through the Ages*, p 50) when he quotes from the grant by Cranmer of, among other items...." all my other rights, franchises, liberties, privileges, profits, commodities, emoluments and all heriditaments whatsoever with their appurtenances....in Harrow, Pynnor, Woodhall....]

1972   The Home Secretary agreed to the changing of the date as suggested in 1967. Under the 1873 Fairs Act, the date became the Wednesday after the last Monday in May. (*Harrow Observer*, 14th February)

1980   "The Showmen's Guild has no authority to restrict the limits of the Fair; it is only the people of Pinner who may decide this. In effect the Fair is owned by the ratepayers. The fact of its being held in the streets has led to objections from local residents and shopkeepers who find it an inconvenience (although it is always held on early closing day.) (Michael Darvell, *Time Out*)

1982   "We all get together to complain about the cost and the smell of the Fair but we come back every year." (Mrs Lampert, *Harrow Observer Midweek*, 8th June)

1983 "I hope the Council and Showmen's Guild will be able to agree on some repositioning of very large equipment for the future." (Chairman, Pinner Association, *The Villager 136*, July 1983)

1984 "Each year more heavy rides were appearing and the Pinner Association asked LBH and the Fire Service to ensure that access for fire engines was kept open. Should the Fair be moved out of the High Street, or indeed out of the centre of Pinner to a site such as the Memorial Park, and should large equipment be banned?" (ib., *The Villager 138*, March 1984)

1985 Councillor Owen Cock stated that there was no reason for Pinner to be disrupted to the extent it had been over the previous five years by progressively earlier arrivals and further encroachments. Following four Fairground accidents, including the death of a 16-year-old girl at Whitley Bay, he called for a full review of the Council's responsibilities and liabilities. The officers of the Council conceded that much of the Fair arrangements rested on custom and long practice. (*Harrow Observer*, 26th September)

"Most people accept the inconvenience and disruption are part of the village life. I see no reason to change it: it gets better." (Mr M Verden)

Councillor Green attacked the moves by Crs. Cock and Bond to restrict the Fair or move it to another site. Gordon Lines for the Chamber of Trade said it would be a terrible thing if this tradition were to change. (*Harrow Observer*, 24th October)

1986 A columnist in *The Observer* repeated the complaints he had heard every year since he was a boy, that the Fair was growing too large, that the machinery was too big for the streets and that it attracted yobs from miles around. The machinery was massive but did no damage. It was bad for trade but lasted only two days. Yobs appeared on the Tube, in football grounds and on all the beaches of Europe, so what was different? There was in fact surprisingly little trouble at the Fair.

Councillors Cock and Bond explained their objections: the emergency services could not get through and they feared what would happen if a helter-skelter toppled over. They would be sorry to see it stopped as it had great historical significance but it was becoming too big. Twenty years ago it was mostly low-level stalls. They suggested a move to Montesole Playing Fields. (*Harrow Observer*, 8th May)

1992 Concern was expressed that the rides were getting so big as to leave no room between each other for access and that they even overlapped the space allocated to other stalls. A fatal accident in 1972 at Battersea Fair, when five people died and fourteen were injured, and another in 1992, when a girl was thrown out of a ride and killed at Margate's Dreamland, were quoted as reasons for concern.

Fair Enough?

Supporters of the Fair queried the logic of moving it to a cricket field at risk to field drains, with no hydrants in case of fire, no street lights, little security and certainly no atmosphere.

At an open meeting organised by the Pinner Association in November, widespread support was expressed for the Fair to be retained in the streets of Pinner. Concern was, however expressed not so much about the safety of the rides themselves as about the lack of emergency exits between the stalls. If people were jammed into a small space, there was nowhere for them to go to allow passage of emergency vehicles. Newly-planted trees, too were seen to be at risk: as they grew larger the showmen were liable to remove branches or otherwise restrict their growth. The new powers of the Health and Safety Executive, were described. Consultations continue.

PINNER FAIR

ACCORDING to Ancient Custom founded upon a Charter granted to the Lord of the Manor and Inhabitants by King Edward the Third in the tenth year of his reign, 1337, and notwithstanding the restrictions and difficulties imposed by the present war—

A FAIR

WILL BE HELD IN

The Streets of Pinner Village

Whitsun-Wednesday, May 31st, 1944

A VARIETY OF PLEASING AMUSEMENTS
will be provided until blackout time.

God Save The King

Pinner Fair carried on even through the War

122

CHAPTER VI

"THE NEXT GAFF"

WE ARE NOT ALONE OR UNIQUE

Practically every town or village in the country seems to have had a Fair at some time. The earliest ones were founded, as is ours, by Royal Charter, which gave official permission to an individual or corporate body to collect rents from stallholders. It is thought likely that many of these grants merely confirmed an existing Fair, some having started, as at Newcastle or Cambridge, in Saxon or even Roman times. Between 1199 and 1400 there were 4860 royal grants of Fairs or Markets. Pinner was merely one of 1560 granted in the 14th century but not many of these still remain. Some of these ancient Fairs were sited where old trade routes crossed, where tool-makers from North Wales could meet wool-sellers from East Anglia or tin-plate workers from the south-west.

The Black Death in 1348 made labour so short that Edward III introduced the Statute of Labourers in 1351, requiring all able-bodied men to present themselves annually for hire at a set wage. These gatherings were reinforced by the Statute of Artificers in 1563 and led to the annual Michaelmas Hiring Fairs (sometimes called 'Statute'' or 'Mop' Fairs). At these, labourers requiring work would parade in the street waiting for prospective employers to choose them in scenes reminiscent of a Roman slave market. Different tradesmen would carry items to identify their calling: a shepherd would carry a 'mop' or tuft of wool, a carter a piece of whipcord, or a milkmaid a tuft of cow's hair. As far as we know, Pinner was never a Hiring Fair for labourers.

The institution of Hiring Fairs was a local business, not the concern of the Crown, and local authorities would have more control over these and their existence than over the Charter Fairs, which required expensive legislation to abolish them.

More recent Fairs have started only when a group of showmen gathered at a plot of vacant ground, such as a town moor, and set up their stalls. These Fairs were often ephemeral and bowed to changing fashions.

Increasing sensibilities in the nineteenth century, and growing awareness of hygiene led to pressures to suppress intemperance, gambling and immorality thought to be encouraged by the heightened excitement of the Fairground. The rising middle-class were anxious to preserve civic amenities, and an untidy sprawl of stalls and roundabouts clashed with this aim: Fairs were seen to be low, vulgar and noisy. Steam-driven organs, in particular, attracted a great deal of opposition as well as generating excitement and drawing in the crowds eager to have a little gaiety in their daily routine. This was especially so in Fairs placed close to residential districts. The Harrow petition of 1859 (see page 99) shows this clearly.

In 1871, Parliament bowed to this pressure with the passing of the Fairs Act, by which the Home Secretary was allowed to abolish any Fair.

Fair Enough?

In Middlesex, a strong weapon was given to the abolitionists in 1909 by the passing of a bye-law "For the Good Rule and Government" of the County. This states that:

> "No person shall in connection with any roundabout show exhibition or performance placed or held in any street or on any vacant ground adjoining or near to a street make or cause to be made any loud and continuous noise by means of any organ or other similar instrument to the annoyance of residents or passengers."　　　　(Public Record Office MEPO/2/5090)

Offenders could be fined up to £2. The bye-law applied to all parts of Middlesex except Municipal Boroughs.

In 1889, a Royal Commission on Markets and Tolls reported after having investigated Fairs and Markets up and down the country. The nearest the Commissioners came to Pinner was to Watford, and they make no mention of Pinner or Harrow Fairs, other than giving the dates of their respective charters. At Watford, they learnt that the Market tolls brought in £55 for the lessee, plus another £82 that he charged for beasts to pass through his private yard on their way to the Market in the open streets.

The commissioners who travelled round the country asked a number of apparently leading questions and the replies they received are summarised in two large Reports. They asked about the local feeling about the Fairs and whether there was any immorality associated with them. Of those whose replies were unambiguous, twenty were strongly opposed and twenty-seven warmly in favour of the continuation of their Pleasure Fairs. A further fifteen places said their Fair was declining in popularity and would wither away of its own accord.

The prize Defender of the Fairs was undoubtedly the Chief Constable of Wigan, who maintained that the Corporation had no right to stop the Fair, as there was "more so-called immorality at a gala got up by the local clergy than at the Fair. The Salvation Army are a greater nuisance than the Fair by parading through the town."

Knowing some of the opposition in Pinner at that time to the Army, we can see his point. They were, of course, the cut-out targets in the Fairground's "Aunt Sally".

Other places in favour of maintaining their Pleasure Fairs were Barnsley, Castleford, Dewsbury, Pontefract and Wombwell in Yorkshire; Barrow, Lancaster, Mossley, Preston and Warrington in Lancashire; and Canterbury in Kent.

The preponderance of votes in favour coming from the north is perhaps worth noting: the middle-class reformists had not so strong a toe-hold there.

At Burnley in Lancashire, the Pleasure Fair had once been removed from the streets, but every market trader had petitioned for it to be revived: in spite of the inconvenience, the increase in trade was considerable during the period of the Fair.

When the Fair at Burslem, Staffs, was stopped in 1879 public opinion forced the authorities to re-start it. Perhaps the £150 a year received by the Council in rents played its part as well. The same reaction occurred in 1883 at St Ives, Huntingdon and at York. When abolition was mooted at Walsall, an overwhelming majority of people voted for their three Fairs to be retained.

Those questioned at Dudley, Worcestershire, reckoned that strong feelings would be aroused there if attempts were made to stop the Fair, as was the case at King's Lynn in Norfolk, where the St Valentine's Day Fair had been going since 1537. There had been some disapproval at Peterborough, but stricter police control and the early closing of public houses, had removed the "worst elements of the Fair". It had once been one of the most important Fairs in the country and in spite of difficulties the residents were loth to see it go. That feeling seems remarkably familiar here. Wolverhampton, too, thought there were fewer complaints than formerly.

"The country people look forward to the Fair for months," said a witness at Loughborough, though here again the drunkenness and the early closing of shops were causes for concern.

Property in Sunderland was said to have depreciated in value once the street Fair had been abolished.

The Commission felt that in general Fairs were becoming improper, and that respectable people had strong objections, but shopkeepers frequently resisted attempts at closure because of the increase in trade.

In their answers to the Commissioners, many towns were non-committal, perhaps weighing up the balance between various classes of voters and conscious of the income from rents and tolls, or perhaps aware of the need to supply "bread and circuses" like the Roman Emperors of old, to keep the lower orders contented.

Some claimed that the Fairs were dying from lack of patronage, as at Doncaster, Stalybridge, Rugby, or Blackburn. Others had already abolished their Pleasure Fairs. These included Bath, Windsor, Whitby, Leeds, St. Helens and Manchester (where the lost income was deeply regretted.)

A Pleasure Fair at Lichfield on Ash Wednesday was by 1888 so small that only £1.50 in modern money was taken in tolls, and the Fair that they said dated back to the time of King Alfred was "not worthwhile for people with steam whistles and organs to come to."

Aylesbury thought a Street Fair was unsuitable for a market town as there were convenient meadows where caravans could go and Hiring Fairs were disliked by modern servants who objected to standing in the streets in public view, waiting to be chosen.

Mansfield found more evil and drunkenness at the time of their November Hiring Fair than at any other. Some of the "shows" then were thought to be improper and "the clangour and row perfectly abominable."

Market Harborough, where the October Fair lasted for ten days, complained not only about the noisy organs but about the lack of hygiene among the travellers. (They gave, incidentally, some interesting details in the course of their evidence: Wombell's

Fair Enough?

menagerie paid a rent of £1, and the coconut shies and shooting galleries 5/- (25p), or 2/6 (12½p).

"At the time the Pleasure Fairs were initiated," stated one witness, "there was a need for them, as present facilities did not exist." Sheffield, too, thought them "antiquated" and would be glad to be rid of them.

Students of election voting patterns could possibly draw some conclusions about the different types of neighbourhoods on either side of the Fairs debate.

But our thoughts keep returning to the Chief Constable of Wigan. Perhaps he was still recalling the words of the Home Secretary in 1884 that there should be no attempt to interfere with the "innocent amusements of the poorer classes."

([Information from the Final Report of the Royal Commission on Market Tolls 1889 Appendix XIV and XXI in Public Record Office)

(See Appendix)

Pinner Fair: the High Street about 1948

THE BIBLIOGRAPHY

Adams, P	*The Fairground* (Child's Play, 1984)
Addison, W	*English Fairs and Markets* (Batsford, 1953)
Anderson, R	*Markets and Fairs of England & Wales* (Bell & Howell, 1985)
Armitage, J	*Man at Play* (Warne, 1977)
Baker, M	*Discovering English Fairs* (Shire, 1965)
Braithwaite, D	*Fairground Architecture* (Evelyn Press, 1968)
	Savage of King's Lynn (Stephens, 1975)
	Travelling Fairs (Shire, 1976)
Brown, F	*Fairfield Folk* (Malvern, 1986)
	Haresfoot Legacy
	Dancing on the Rainbow
	Other Sister (Headline Books, 1990)
Cockayne, E	*Fairground Organs* (David & Charles, n/d)
Crawley, J	*Fairground Organs in Focus* (Crawley, 1983)
Dallas, D	*The Travelling People* (Macmillan, 1971)
Dexter, F T G	*The Pagan Origin of Fairs* (New Knowledge Press, 1930)
Dillon, R C	*A Sermon on the Evils of Fairs* (London, 1830)
Disher, M W	*Fairs, Circuses and Music Halls* (Collins, 1942)
Dormer, J	*Markets and Fairs* (Wayland, 1973)
Douglas-Irvine, H	*Extracts Relating to Mediaeval Markets & Fairs in England* (Macdonald & Evans, 1912)
Downie, G	*All the Fun of the Fair* (Showmen's Guild, 1987)
Drake, Sir H G T	*The English Circus and Fairground* (Methuen, 1946)
Druett, W	*Pinner Through the Ages* (Ringstead Press, 1980)
Elton & Costelloe	*Royal Commission on Market Rights and Tolls* (HMSO 1889)
Fay, A	*Bioscope Shows and Their Engines* (Oakwood Press, 1966)
Fried, F	*A Pictorial History of the Carousel* (Barnes, New York, 1965)
Frost, T	*The Old Showmen and Old London Fairs* (Tinsley, 1874)
Gaches, L	*The Law Relating to Markets & Fairs* (1898)
Gadsden, E (Ed)	*The Panorama of Pinner Village* (Pinner Association, 1969)
Golland, J (Ed)	*When I Was a Child* (PLHS 1984)
Jacob, J	*The Compleat Parish Officer* (6th Edn., Lintot & Birt, 1731)
Johnston, M	*Fairground Family* (Black, 1985)
Jonson, B	*Bartholomew Fayre* (1614)
	The Alchemist (1610)
McKechnie, S	*Popular Entertainment Through the Ages* (Sampson Low, 1931)
Miller, D N	*Fairground & Circus Transport* (Roundabout, 1990)
Miller, D P	*The Life of a Showman* (1849)
Moore, E	*The Fairs of Mediaeval England* (Canada, 1985)
Morley, H	*Memoirs of Bartholomew Fair* (Chapman Hall, 1859)
Moss, M	*Fairs & Circuses* (Wayland, 1986)
Muncey, R W	*Our Old English Fairs* (Sheldon Press, 1936)
Owen, W	*(New) Book of Fairs* (1753-1888)
Price, M R	*A Portrait of the Middle Ages* (OUP, 1951)
Purton, R M	*Markets and Fairs* (Routledge, Kegan & Paul, 1973)
Roope, F C	*Come to the Fair (Showmen's Guild, 1961)*
Sanger, G	*Seventy Years a Showman* (McGibbon & Kee, 1966)
Starsmore, I	*The Fairground* (Whitechapel Art Gallery, 1977)
	English Fairs (Thames & Hudson, 1973)
Taylor, V	*Reminiscences of a Showman* (Allen Lane,)
Torre, H J	*Recollections of Schooldays at Harrow more than 50 Years Ago* (Charles Simons, 1890)
Walford, C	*Fairs Past and Present* (Elliot Stock, 1883)
Ware, E M	*Pinner in the Vale* (Pinner Press, 1955)
Ware, M E	*Historic Fairground Scenes* (Moorland, 1977)
Weedon & Ward	*Fairground Art* (Millways, 1985)
White, P	*Fairs and Circuses* (Black, 1972)
Wilkins, F	*Fairs* (Blackwell, 1969)
?	*Markets and Fairs* (Hertfordshire Record Office)

(Note: Not many of these books are readily available, even through the splendid efforts of the local Borough Library Services. Most, though, can be seen in the British Library.)

Fair Enough?

FAIRS OF MIDDLESEX

William Owen, the bookseller, published regular lists of *The Fairs of England* and Wales from 1756 onwards. His successors produced the last one in 1888. None of these mention Pinner, Harrow or Hillingdon Fairs. They include, at various times, the following in Middlesex:

BOW	Three days in Whit week for toys
BEGGARS'S BUSH	September 12 for horses and toys
BRENTFORD	May 17 - 19; September 12 - 14 for horses, cattle, hogs; Charter allowed six days for each
CHISWICK	July 15 - 17 for toys
EDGWARE	Holy Thursday: horses and cows (or May 4)
EDMONTON	September 14 - 16 for hiring and toys
ENFIELD	Charter 1302; September 23 for hiring; November 30 for horses, cows and cheese
HAMMERSMITH	May 1 for toys
HOUNSLOW	Charter 1295; Trinity Monday; Monday after September 29 for cattle & sheep
LONDON	St Bartholomew's in Smithfield: Charter 1133; suppressed 1855; September 4 for toys
STAINES	May 11 for horses & cattle; Statute (hiring) Fair September 19 for onions & toys
TWICKENHAM	Holy Thursday; Monday & Tuesday before Michaelmas
UXBRIDGE	Statute Fair March 25; July 31; Hiring Fair September 29; October 10 for horses, cows & sheep; flourished from 1612 at least
WALHAM GREEN	June 24 for toys

(In addition, BARNET is included under Middlesex in 1756)

In his *Book of Roads*, Owen includes Pinner as being two miles from Harrow and fifteen from London, so his request in an early edition for him to be informed if "any small errors have crept in" seems justified.

As well as the above, the following Fairs in Middlesex have been noted. There may well be others:

ACTON	Whitsun Carnival 1992
BRENT	Show, August 21 - 31, 1992
COLNBROOK	July, mid-19th century
EDGWARE	August 1, three days; for cattle & pleasure

FINCHLEY	Carnival, July 1992
FULHAM	Fair July 1992
HACKNEY DOWNS	Fairs 1961 - 92
HAMPSTEAD HEATH	Easter Monday; Whit Monday; in Upper & Lower Heath & Vale of Heath
HAMPTON COURT	Easter
HAREFIELD	Mid-19th century
HARROW	Founded 1260/1; confirmed 1315; held in main road on September 7 - 9; protests 1859; held latterly on first Monday in August at request of Harrow School; abolished 1872
HILLINGDON	Mid-May, at least from 1883 - 1992
HYDE PARK	In 1838 to celebrate Coronation of Queen Victoria; roundabouts at each corner
ICKENHAM	In 19th century, by pond
PINNER	Founded 1336 for June 23 - 25 & August 28 - 29; then Whit Wednesday; now Wednesday after Spring Bank Holiday
KINGSBURY	Roe Green:May 1992
RUISLIP	On Ascension Day until 1939, by The George; also sports day
"SKRINE"	Charter 1330
WEMBLEY	Barham Park August 14 - 16, 1992

GLOSSARY

Build-up	The erection of the stalls, shows and rides
Gaff	A stall or ride
Gaffer	A riding-master, one in charge
Josser	A lay-man, an outsider and not a traveller
Juveniles	Roundabouts or other rides designed for young children
Pull-down	The dismantling of the Fair
Sidestuff	Stalls, smaller shows and snack-bars
Smasher	A passer of false coinage
Sounding Boards	Decorated fringe below the tilts
Swifts	Wooden spokes forming the roof of a ride
Tickler (Tiddler)	Cardboard tube with feathers used for teasing others
Tilts	Awning of a roundabout or other ride
Tober	The Fairground (or the open road)

Fair Enough?

INDEX

Fair Enough?